fresh and healthy

# juices

# fresh and healthy juices

## Nature's cure-all
## for health and vitality

# Jan Castorina & Dimitra Stais

SIMON &
SCHUSTER

London · New York · Sydney · Toronto

A CBS COMPANY

# Contents

# All About Juices

An amazing array of fresh fruit and vegetable juices are available today, offering both a refreshing taste and a wide variety of nutrients. Not only do juices contain vitamins and minerals, but also live enzymes and other nutrients that are revitalizing and health-giving. Most important of all, juices taste wonderful and make us feel great.

This book will show you how to improve and maintain your health by drinking fresh juices every day. It includes many kinds of extracted juices, blended drinks and infusions, and their therapeutic applications.

Use the Ailment Index to find the drink suited to your health concern. There are drinks designed specifically for women, for boosting energy, for improving immunity, and for detoxifying. We have created drinks specifically for different family members and for those who are watching their calorie intake.

While we may suggest particular juices for certain health conditions or age groups, most of our drinks are suitable for anyone at any time. We suggest that you also experiment with different flavor combinations of your favorite fruits and vegetables.

If any of the juices seem too strong, simply dilute them with pure water. Vegetable juices for children should always be diluted, as children have more delicate digestive systems. Anyone with a blood-sugar disorder should also dilute fruit juices to cut down on the amount of fructose, or natural fruit sugar. Whole, low-fat or nonfat milk or fortified soy milk may be used in any of the recipes that call for milk.

Unless otherwise specified, we have not peeled, seeded, corded or deveined our ingredients. For most juice extractors this is unnecessary and, more importantly, many nutrients lie within the skin of fruits and vegetables. For this reason, wherever possible use fresh organic fruit and vegetables to minimize the intake of pesticides and artificial fertilizers. If you do not have access to organic produce, wash your fruit and vegetables very well in biodegradable detergent to shift any pesticide residue, then rinse thoroughly before use.

When chopping fruit and vegetables for processing in a juice extractor, cut them into pieces small enough to fit the extractor opening—they do not need to be finely chopped. Small foods, such as ginger, do not need to be cut smaller if they fit easily into the opening.

While we have recommended particular combinations of juices and other ingredients for specific health problems, these drinks are intended only to supply nutrients that may be beneficial and are not to be used as treatment for these conditions. It is important to seek qualified professional advice for any health concern.

We hope you enjoy our drinks as much as we enjoyed researching, developing and tasting them with our friends.

# Extraction Methods

To make the drinks in this book, you will need a blender, a juice extractor, and a citrus juicer. The blender is used to make fruit smoothies and drinks from soft fruits such as bananas, persimmons and passion fruits. To make juice from hard fruits and vegetables, you will need a juice extractor. Citrus fruits can be juiced easily with any kind of citrus juicer.

## Blenders

There are many blenders available, varying in size and power. When choosing one, check the motor size, how easy it is to clean and reassemble, and whether it has more than one speed. Some come with a handy grinder for coffee beans or for nuts and seeds. Although blenders range in price, you should invest in a good-quality one that will last for years without problems.

## Juice extractors

If you intend to make juices a regular part of your life, it is worth investing in a good-quality juice extractor. Make sure you shop around and ask about the features of each machine: how it operates, what style it is, how it is cleaned, the size of the motor and, of course, the price. All these points will help you determine which kind to purchase. The following are the three main types of juice extractors, as determined by the kind of motor that powers them:

**Centrifugal extractors:** This type of extractor finely grates food and uses centrifugal force to expel the extracted juice into a container. These extractors either allow the pulp to accumulate within the machine's container or expel the pulp into another container. The benefit of the latter type is that you don't have to stop and empty out the pulp quite as often. A centrifugal motor tends to add oxygen to juices, which can decrease their keeping time as oxygen destroys certain vitamins. If you have this style of extractor, always drink your juices immediately to gain the most nutrients.

**Masticating extractors:** More expensive than the centrifugal type, the masticating extractor finely grates the food and then "chews" it to make even finer particles. It then presses the pulp to extract the juices, expelling the pulp after the juice is extracted. It doesn't incorporate oxygen into the juices, so it provides high-quality juice which will keep for a day in a refrigerator.

**Hydraulic press extractors:** The most expensive and most efficient type. This machine grates food, then crushes it with revolving cutters. The pulp is put under tremendous pressure to extract all the juice, leaving a very dry pulp. This extractor makes juice with the highest amount of nutrients and doesn't incorporate oxygen during the process. Juices made with this type of extractor can be stored in airtight containers in the refrigerator for a day or two.

## Citrus Juicers

These are available in a wide variety, from simple manual juicers to electric ones. They all do more or less the same job, and the type you purchase will depend on your taste and budget.

# Vitamins & Minerals

## Their Functions and Food Sources

| Vitamin | Functions | Food Sources |
| --- | --- | --- |
| Vitamin A (retinol/beta-carotene) | Beta-carotene is converted into vitamin A in the body as needed for good vision, growth and development. It is also an important antioxidant. | Vitamin A: Liver, fish liver oils, butter and margarine, egg yolks.<br>Beta-carotene: All orange, red and green fruits and vegetables; leafy herbs. |
| Vitamin B1 (thiamin) | Needed for the metabolism of carbohydrates, nervous system function and heart function. | Yeast, yeast spreads such as marmite, promite or vegemite, whole grains, milk, yogurt. |
| Vitamin B2 (riboflavin) | Needed for metabolism and growth. | Yeast, milk, yogurt, whole grains, fortified breakfast cereals, eggs, meats. |
| Vitamin B3 (niacin) | Needed for the nervous system, the manufacture of fatty acids and neurotransmitters, healthy skin and as an aid for digestion. | Yeast, meats, poultry, breads, fortified breakfast cereals, nuts, legumes, potatoes. |
| Vitamin B5 (pantothenic acid) | Needed for the synthesis of cholesterol and fat, the metabolism of major nutrients, the release of energy, tissue growth and adrenal function. | All vegetables, meat, rice, dried fruit and nuts, liver, bran. |
| Vitamin B6 (pyridoxine) | Needed for immune function; the metabolism of fat, protein and carbohydrates; energy release, nervous system and red blood cells. | Yeast, yeast extracts such as marmite, promite or vegemite, nuts, bananas, eggs, whole-grain (wholemeal) bread, cereals, soybeans, avocados, legumes, meats, liver, fish, poultry. |
| Vitamin B12 (cyanocobalamin) | Essential for DNA and RNA, myelin sheaths on nerves, red blood cells, cell division and folate transport. | Animal products such as meat, poultry, eggs, fish and dairy, as well as miso, mushrooms, spirulina. |
| Folate (folic acid) | For cell division, DNA and RNA, the metabolism of protein, red blood cells and for early pregnancy to prevent neural tube defects. | Green leafy vegetables and herbs, broccoli, Brussels sprouts, oranges, corn, bananas, avocados, wheat germ, legumes, whole grains, yeast, liver. |
| Vitamin C (ascorbic acid, calcium ascorbate, sodium ascorbate) | Needed for collagen formation, antioxidant activity, healthy bones and teeth, blood-vessel maintenance, neurotransmitter function, detoxification and immune function; aids iron absorption (from plant sources). | Citrus fruit, guava, fresh coconut water, kiwifruit, bell peppers (capsicum), black currants, potatoes, broccoli, rose hips, parsley and all other fruits and vegetables. |
| Vitamin D (calciferol) | Promotes healthy bones and teeth by aiding the absorption of calcium and phosphorus. | Eggs, fish liver oils, tuna, salmon, sardines; made by the body during exposure to sunlight. |

| Vitamin | Functions | Food Sources |
| --- | --- | --- |
| Vitamin E (tocopherol) | Needed for antioxidant activity, the protection of fatty acids, detoxification and for healthy red blood cells and body tissues. | Wheat germ, wheat germ oil, nuts, seeds, avocados, egg yolks, tuna, seed oils, broccoli. |
| Vitamin K | Needed for correct blood clotting and bone protection. | Dark green leafy vegetables, broccoli, Brussels sprouts, liver. |
| Calcium | Needed for healthy bones and teeth, nerve transmission, muscle function and nerve function. | Milk and dairy, canned sardines and salmon (with bones), green leafy vegetables, sesame seeds, carob powder, nuts (especially almonds and Brazil nuts), seeds, tofu made with a calcium-based setting agent, dried figs. |
| Chromium | Needed for the regulation of blood sugar levels and plays a role in cholesterol regulation. | Yeast, kiwifruit, egg yolks, cereals, red meats, liver, seafood, whole grains, molasses, cheese. |
| Iodine | Plays an essential role in thyroid hormone production and metabolic rate regulation. | Iodized table salt, kelp, spirulina, seaweed, seafood, cheese, milk, meats, cereals. |
| Iron | Needed for hemoglobin production and enzyme production for energy. | Dried apricots, egg yolks, dark green leafy vegetables, meats (especially organ meats—offal), legumes, chicken, fish. |
| Magnesium | Needed for healthy bones and teeth, healthy muscle function and contraction, nerve impulses and neurotransmitters. | Nuts, seeds, dried figs, wheat germ, legumes, whole grains, green vegetables, seafood, meat. |
| Manganese | Promotes enzyme function for energy production, healthy bones & healthy connective tissue. | Nuts, whole grains, legumes, brown rice. |
| Phosphorus | For healthy bones, teeth, energy release and nutrient absorption; works with B vitamins. | All plant and animal foods. |
| Potassium | Needed for correct electrolyte balance in cells (works with sodium), healthy blood pressure, blood volume and heart function and nerve transmission. | Celery, celery root (celeriac), bananas, tomatoes, dried fruit, potatoes, nuts, avocados, legumes, seeds, citrus, most unprocessed foods. |
| Selenium | Promotes antioxidant activity, immune function and sexual development. | Brazil nuts, meats, fish, dairy foods, avocados, lentils, cereals. |
| Sodium | Corrects electrolyte balance in cells; aids healthy heart function, blood pressure and blood volume (works with potassium), and muscle function. | Table salt, sea salt, yeast extract, processed foods. It is found in good proportions with other nutrients in unprocessed foods such as vegetables and grains. |
| Zinc | Immune function, enzyme action, growth and reproduction, neurotransmitters and insulin synthesis. | Oysters, peanuts, sunflower seeds, pumpkin seeds (pepitas), red meat, eggs, legumes, organ meats (offal), cereals, nuts. |

# Energy Boosters

How often do you need an energy boost? At these times do you reach for chocolate or coffee? Many people fall into the trap of choosing sugar- or caffeine-loaded foods and drinks to give themselves an energy kick. When you do this often, however, it can affect your general health. Too much sugar can cause an imbalance within your blood sugar levels, and caffeine is a drug and should not be relied upon for its ability to increase alertness.

Instead of choosing foods that will eventually reduce your energy level, reach for juices and other drinks to get a natural energy boost. As a bonus, fresh juices and fruits contain all manner of wonderful nutrients that promote good health. At mealtimes, you should eat a good balance of carbohydrate foods, such as bread, pasta, rice, potatoes or other similar foods, along with a protein food such as meat, chicken, fish, legumes, eggs or tofu, and lots of raw or cooked vegetables as nutritious meals will keep your energy levels up. Fresh fruit and nuts and seeds eaten daily also provide essential nutrients.

The drinks in this chapter can be enjoyed at any time and by everyone, but they are also designed for specific times and needs, such as for breakfast, afternoon snacks, sports and general fatigue. You will even find a drink to have before and after a big night out, as well as those to improve concentration for studying or working late and to help you recover from jet lag.

To share the drinks with family or friends, multiply the recipes accordingly.

*Fast Breakfast Drink*
(*see* page 14)

## Fast Breakfast Drink

~

For a nutritious breakfast that can be made in a flash. This drink provides many essential nutrients such as carbohydrate, protein, vitamin E, B vitamins including B6 and folate, and zinc and magnesium. The yogurt provides friendly bacteria, which help to boost immunity.

~

*Makes about 2½ cups
(20 fl oz/625 ml); serves 2*
~

*1 cup (8 fl oz/250 ml) milk
or fortified soy milk, chilled
¼ cup (2 oz/60g) natural
acidophilus yogurt
4 oz (125 g) fresh strawberries,
hulled, or thawed frozen
strawberries
2 medium passion fruit, halved and
flesh scooped from peel
2 teaspoons wheat germ
2 teaspoons honey or sugar*

In a blender, combine all the ingredients and process until smooth. Serve immediately.

## Pineapple and Ginger Lifter

~

This is a good drink to have while working or studying, as the enzymes in pineapple help to keep you alert and aid concentration. The ginger and mint add a little zing to this drink.

~

*Makes about 1 cup
(8 fl oz/250 ml); serves 1*
~

*¾-inch (2-cm) piece fresh ginger
½ medium pineapple, peeled, cored
and chopped
½ teaspoon finely chopped fresh
mint*

In a juice extractor, process the ginger, then the pineapple. Stir in the mint.

## Carrot, Tomato and Cucumber Juice

~

A good drink for when you have to work late. The basil helps concentration and aids digestion. Tomato juice provides nutrients that help to stimulate the circulation, and cucumber helps you to stay alert.

~

*Makes about 1¼ cups
(10 fl oz/310 ml); serves 1*
~

*2 medium carrots, chilled
and chopped
1 small tomato, chilled
and chopped
1 small cucumber, chilled and
chopped
5–6 large fresh basil leaves,
finely chopped*

In a juice extractor, process the carrots, tomato, and cucumber. Pour into a glass, stir in the basil and drink immediately.

*Pineapple and Ginger Lifter*

## Strawberry and Pineapple Pick-me-up

~

An energy booster to try when you're feeling fatigued, this drink supplies magnesium, vitamin C and potassium, along with enzymes to aid digestion. The alfalfa sprouts act as a tonic and contains chlorophyll, which has a cleansing quality.

~

*Makes about 1¼ cups (10 fl oz/310 ml); serves 1*

~

*1 oz (30 g) alfalfa sprouts*
*1 kiwifruit, chopped*
*4 oz (125 g) fresh strawberries, hulled, or frozen strawberries*
*¼ medium pineapple, peeled, cored, and chopped*

In a juice extractor, process the alfalfa, then the kiwifruit, strawberries and pineapple.

## Kiwi, Apple and Grape Lifter

~

A boost of natural fruit sugar can help to raise your energy level in the afternoon while you're busy at work or at home. As a bonus, the kiwifruit contains lots of vitamin C and enzymes; the apple contains pectin, vitamin C and ellagic acid (an anti-cancer agent); and the grapes supply flavonoids, which act as antioxidants.

~

*Makes about 1¼ cups (10 fl oz/310 ml); serves 1*

~

*1 kiwifruit, chopped*
*1 small apple, chopped*
*7 oz (220 g) red grapes*

Process all the ingredients in a juice extractor. Mix well.

## Guava and Pineapple Kick-starter

~

Have this drink when you need to give your immune system a quick boost, such as after a long aeroplane trip or other tiring journey. Guava is high in vitamin C, and pineapple contains vitamin C as well as enzymes beneficial for digestion. If guava is not available, use kiwifruit instead, as they are also high in vitamin C and enzymes.

~

*Makes about 1½ cups (12 fl oz/375 ml); serves 1–2*

~

*¼ medium pineapple, cored, peeled and chopped*
*1 large guava, cut into thin wedges*

In a juice extractor, process the pineapple and guava, mix well.

*Strawberry and Pineapple Pick-me-up* (right)
*Kiwi, Apple and Grape Lifter* (left)

# Banana and Apricot Thick Shake

~

Try this drink for a quick boost of energy needed for fast sports, such as squash, sprinting, rowing and dancing. The banana and apricots provide plenty of complex carbohydrates, and the milk and yogurt provide calcium and protein. The apricots also supply beta-carotene and iron, which are needed to support the body during exercise.

~

*Makes about 2¾ cups
(22 fl oz/680 ml); serves 2–3*

~

10 dried apricots (about 2½ oz/75g)
1½ cups (12 fl oz /375 ml) milk or
fortified soy milk, chilled
½ cup (4 oz/125 g) natural
acidophilus yogurt or soy yogurt
1 medium banana, peeled
2 teaspoons honey
4 ice cubes

Put the apricots in a small bowl and add boiling water to cover. Let sit for 15 minutes. Drain and let cool to room temperature. In a blender, combine the apricots with all the remaining ingredients and process until smooth. Serve immediately.

# Raisin–Cocoa Shake

~

When you are about to do extended exercise, such as a long, strenuous walk or triathlon training, you need a high-energy food. Raisins and milk add carbohydrate to this shake, while cocoa and orange add a flavor boost.

~

*Makes about 1 cup
(8 fl oz/250 ml); serves 1*

~

2 oz (60 g) golden raisins
(sultanas)
1 cup (8 fl oz/250 ml) cold milk or
fortified soy milk, chilled
1 tablespoon unsweetened cocoa
powder
1 teaspoon finely grated orange zest
1 teaspoon sugar

Put the raisins in a small saucepan and add water to cover. Bring to a boil over medium-high heat, reduce heat to medium-low, cover and cook for 10 minutes. Drain and let cool to room temperature. In a blender, combine the raisins and all the remaining ingredients and blend until smooth.

# Date and Plum Soy Shake

~

A great energy booster for skiing or other winter sports, this warming drink can also be made with cold milk, if you prefer. Dates contain magnesium, which is needed for the release of energy and to avoid muscle fatigue and cramps. They are also high in potassium to replace any loss due to perspiration. Soy milk provides carbohydrate and fatty acids needed for energy. The plums add sweetness and flavor and also contain some magnesium and potassium.

~

*Makes about 1½ cups
(12 fl oz/375 ml); serves 1–2*

~

6 dates, pitted and chopped
¼ cup (2 fl oz/60 ml) water
2 canned dark plums in natural
juice, drained, halved, and pitted
¾ cup (6 fl oz/180 ml) hot soy milk

In a small saucepan, combine the dates and water. Bring to a boil, stirring until the mixture forms a paste. Spoon into a blender. Add the plums and soy milk and blend until smooth. Serve immediately.

*Banana and Apricot Thick Shake*

## Mango and Strawberry Shake

~

This drink is excellent for kids playing sports. The fruits provide energy, while the ice cream and milk or soy milk slow the release of the fructose, making this an energy-sustaining drink. The milk or soy milk also provides calcium.

~

*Makes about 2 cups*
*(16 fl oz/500 ml); serves 1–2*

~

*½ mango, peeled and fruit cut from the pit*
*4 oz (125 g) fresh strawberries, hulled, or thawed frozen strawberries*
*1 scoop (about 1 oz/30 g) low-fat ice cream*
*1 cup (8 fl oz/250 ml) milk or fortified soy milk*

In a blender, combine all the ingredients and blend until smooth. Serve immediately.

## Tomato and Celery Juice

~

This high-potassium drink is excellent when you have been perspiring heavily while doing heavy manual work. The potassium in the celery and tomato combined with the salt in the Worcestershire sauce will help to rebalance the electrolytes in your circulatory system.

~

*Makes about 1 cup*
*(8 fl oz/250 ml); serves 1*

~

*1 celery stalk with leaves, chopped*
*⅔ cup (5 fl oz/160 ml) tomato juice, chilled*
*½ teaspoon Worcestershire sauce*

In a juice extractor, process the celery. Pour the celery juice into a glass and stir in the tomato juice and Worcestershire.

## Red Pepper Booster

~

This is a drink to have before and after a big night. The grapefruit is naturally bitter, so if you prefer a sweeter drink, use orange juice. The vitamin C in the pepper and the citrus juice assists in detoxifying your body from alcohol, while the beet provides potassium, magnesium and beta-carotene to help reduce fatigue and replace essential nutrients. Dilute this drink with some water if you prefer.

~

*Makes about 1¼ cups*
*(10 fl oz/310 ml); serves 1*

~

*½ medium beet (beetroot), chopped*
*½ medium red bell pepper (capsicum), chopped*
*1 medium grapefruit or orange, peeled and chopped*

In a juice extractor, process first the beet, then the pepper and grapefruit or orange.

*Mango and Strawberry Shake*

# Immune Boosters

There are many times during our lives when we can benefit from a boost to our immune system. Our busy, stressful lifestyles call for extra care to keep immune function at its best. Apart from adopting a healthy diet, you can help immune function by exercising regularly—just a 30-minute walk a day does wonders—drinking plenty of pure water, and taking time out to rest and relax each day. If you are too ill to go for walks, simple stretching exercises will help to improve your lymphatic circulation, which in turn improves immune function.

Meditation practice in a formal or informal way also helps to improve immunity. Laughing has always been called the best medicine, and this is not a joke as it really helps to have a good belly laugh regularly. Why not rent a funny movie, or get together with friends and play some silly games together or just have a laugh. If you live alone, consider keeping a pet. Having a furry or feathery friend to look after makes a tremendous difference in people's lives—it decreases stress, helps increase immune function and reduces feelings of loneliness.

Fresh air and contact with nature, such as being by the sea or a river, or among the trees in a forest, also helps to improve health. When in contact with nature, take time to breathe deeply and allow yourself to rest and reflect.

The drinks in this chapter are designed to help your immune system to function better in different situations. You will find drinks for colds and flu, allergies, chronic fatigue syndrome and HIV, as well as for before and after surgery, for chronic illness or convalescence, to prevent cancer, and for stress.

*Black Currant and Orange Egg-flip* (*see* page 26)

## Hot Lemon Drink

~

This is an excellent drink when you have a cold or flu, or feel one coming on. The lemon provides vitamin C, and the ginger and chili powder help to clear the sinuses. Honey soothes a sore throat. When making this drink for a child, dilute it with more hot water and reduce or omit the chili powder.

~

*Makes about 1 cup*
*(8 fl oz/250 ml); serves 1*

~

*¾ cup (6 fl oz/180 ml) boiling*
*water*
*1 teaspoon grated lemon zest*
*¼ cup (2 fl oz/60 ml) fresh lemon*
*juice*
*1 teaspoon grated fresh ginger*
*3 teaspoons honey, or to taste*
*Pinch of chili powder or cayenne*
*pepper*

In a mug, combine all the ingredients and stir to blend. Serve hot.

## Citrus Cold and Flu Fighter

~

This wicked-sounding brew does the job. Onion and garlic are excellent expectorants and help to break up congestion, and garlic is a strong natural antibiotic. The citrus fruits provide vitamin C to help boost the immune system, and honey soothes a sore throat.

~

*Makes about ⅔ cup*
*(5 fl oz/160 ml); serves 1*

~

*1 small clove garlic*
*⅛ chopped red (Spanish) onion*
*½ medium lemon, peeled*
*and chopped*
*1 medium orange, peeled*
*and chopped*
*½ teaspoon honey, or to taste*

In a juice extractor, process first the garlic, then the onion, lemon and orange. Add the honey and whisk to combine.

## Smooth Orange Healer

~

After you have had a virus, you need lots of nutrients to boost your immune system and bring you back to good health. This drink contains vitamin C, which is usually depleted during a virus, as well as beta-carotene, bioflavonoids, a natural antibiotic from the garlic, B vitamins from the yeast and more.

~

*Makes about 1 cup*
*(8 fl oz/250 ml); serves 1*

~

*1 clove garlic*
*¾ oz (20 g) fresh parsley sprigs*
*8 oz (250 g) paw-paw or papaya,*
*peeled, seeded, and chopped*
*1 orange, peeled and chopped*
*½ teaspoon brewer's yeast (optional,*
*to taste)*

In a juice extractor, process first the garlic, then the parsley, paw-paw and orange. Whisk in the brewer's yeast, if using.

*Hot Lemon Drink*

24

## Lemon, Carrot and Orange Juice

~

A juice for sufferers of chronic fatigue syndrome—the lemon stimulates gallbladder and liver function while the carrot helps boost the immune system.

~

*Makes about 1 cup*
*(8 fl oz/250 ml); serves 1*
~
*1 orange, peeled and chopped*
*½ lemon, peeled and chopped*
*2 medium carrots, chopped*

In a juice extractor, process all the ingredients and mix well. Drink immediately.

## Black Currant and Orange Egg-flip

~

This drink is full of good-quality nutrients for the chronically ill. It is easy to drink and provides protein from the egg and milk, flavonoids from the currants and B vitamins from yeast.

~

*Makes about 1¼ cups*
*(10 fl oz/310 ml): serves 1*
~
*¾ cup (6 fl oz/180 ml) milk or fortified soy milk, chilled*
*3.5 oz (100 g) frozen black currants or other berries, thawed*
*1 egg*
*¼ cup (2 fl oz/60 ml) water*
*2 teaspoons honey, or to taste*
*1 teaspoon grated orange zest*
*½ teaspoon brewer's yeast*

In a blender, combine all the ingredients and blend until very smooth.

## Pineapple, Carrot and Broccoli Immune Enhancer

~

For those with HIV or a chronic viral illness, it is very important to enhance immune function. Carotenes and vitamin C help achieve this and are plentiful in this drink. Zinc can also benefit, so sunflower and pumpkin seeds should be eaten daily for their zinc content.

~

*Makes about 1¼ cups*
*(10 fl oz/310 ml); serves 1*
~
*¼ medium pineapple, peeled, cored and chopped*
*1 medium carrot, chopped*
*4 oz (125 g) chopped broccoli*

In a juice extractor, process all the ingredients. Drink immediately.

## Orange Sweet Potato and Spinach Juice

~

For those suffering from chronic fatigue or exhaustion, this drink provides vitamin C, needed for stress and illness; carotenes to boost immune function; and B vitamins and folate, needed to cope with stress and tiredness.

~

*Makes about 1 cup*
*(8 fl oz/250 ml); serves 1*
~
*1 large (about 1¾ lb/875 g) orange sweet potato, peeled and chopped*
*1 large orange, peeled and chopped*
*2½ oz (75 g) fresh spinach leaves*

Process all the ingredients in a juice extractor. Mix well and drink immediately.

*Orange Sweet Potato and Spinach Juice*

## Chlorophyll-boost Juice

~

When you are chronically ill, your system can often do with a gentle cleanse and some good-quality nutrients. This drink provides plenty of chlorophyll, which is an excellent internal cleanser, and folate, which can assist with depression; and the spirulina provides excellent nutrients like protein, vitamin B12 and natural iron.

~

*Makes about 1¼ cups*
*(10 fl oz/310 ml); serves 1*

~

*2 large apples, chopped*
*3.5 oz (100 g) chopped broccoli*
*½–1 teaspoon spirulina, to taste*

In a juice extractor, process the apples and broccoli. Whisk in the spirulina and drink immediately.

## Pear, Licorice and Orange Drink

~

This juice is an anti-inflammatory drink that combines the anti-allergy and inflammation-reducing qualities of licorice with orange zest for its natural bioflavonoids. Pear juice, which is tolerated by most people with allergies, supplies some vitamin C.

~

*Makes about 1 cup*
*(8 fl oz/250 ml); serves 1*

~

*2 teaspoons dried licorice*
*root, chopped*
*¼ cup (2 fl oz/60 ml) boiling water*
*1 large pear, cut into thin wedges*
*1 teaspoon finely grated orange zest*

In a small bowl, combine the licorice and boiling water. Cover and let steep for 10 minutes. Strain, reserving the liquid. In a juice extractor, process the pear. Combine with the licorice tea and orange zest and mix well.

## Carrot, Bell Pepper and Lime Juice

~

This juice provides antioxidants—beta-carotene, flavonoids and vitamin C—which reduce the free-radical activity that can promote cancer growth.

~

*Makes about 1¼ cups*
*(10 fl oz/310 ml); serves 1*

~

*2 medium carrots, chopped*
*½ large red bell pepper (capsicum),*
*seeded and chopped*
*Finely grated zest and juice of*
*1 lime*

In a juice extractor, process the carrots and bell pepper. Combine with the lime zest and juice and mix well.

*Chlorophyll-boost Juice*

## Refreshing Grapefruit Lifter

~

Winter can make you feel a bit blue, but this fresh-tasting drink will help to lift your spirits, improve your digestion and boost your immune system with a good hit of vitamin C. Fennel and ginger also help to clear the sinuses.

~

*Makes about 1 cup*
*(8 fl oz/250 ml); serves 1*

~

*¾-inch (2-cm) piece fresh ginger*
*1 medium fennel bulb, chopped*
*½ medium apple, chopped*
*11 oz (340 g) pink or regular grapefruit, peeled and chopped*

In a juice extractor, process first the ginger, then the fennel, apple and grapefruit.

## Lemon Balm and Pineapple Drink

~

This is a lovely drink to have when you are about to travel. Pineapple helps to keep you alert, lemon balm reduces pre-travel stress, and ginger helps to prevent motion sickness.

~

*Makes about 1 cup*
*(8 fl oz/250 ml); serves 1*

~

*1 lemon balm tea bag*
*¼ cup (2 fl oz/60 ml) boiling water*
*¾-inch (2-cm) piece fresh ginger, peeled and chopped*
*¼ medium pineapple, peeled, cored and chopped*

Put the tea bag in a mug and add the hot water. Let steep for 15 minutes, then remove the tea bag. In a juice extractor, process first the ginger, then the pineapple. Pour in the tea and whisk to combine.

## Ginseng and Apricot Drink

~

Ginseng is an excellent herb to help you deal with stress. Combined with yogurt and apricots, it makes an energy booster with some friendly bacteria to help improve digestion, a common side effect of stress.

~

*Makes about 1½ cups*
*(12 fl oz/375 ml); serves 1–2*

~

*2.5 oz (75 g) dried apricots*
*1 ginseng tea bag or sachet*
*1 cup (8 fl oz/250 ml) boiling water*
*½ cup (4 oz/125 g) natural acidophilus yogurt*

Put the apricots in a bowl and add the contents of the tea bag or sachet. Add the boiling water and let sit for 15 minutes. Refrigerate until chilled, about 30 minutes. In a blender, combine the apricot mixture and yogurt and blend until smooth.

*Refreshing Grapefruit Lifter*

## Super Orange Booster

~

Full of vitamin C, folate and beta-carotene, this drink helps to boost immune function and would be good to take before having surgery. It's a deliciously sweet drink, and the lemon balm helps to promote calmness and serenity.

~

*Makes about 1 cup*
*(8 fl oz/250 ml); serves 1*

~

½ *mango, peeled and cut from*
*the pit*
*1 orange, peeled and chopped*
*1 carrot, chopped*
½ *teaspoon finely chopped fresh lemon balm*

In a juice extractor, process the mango, orange and carrot. Whisk in the lemon balm.

## Orange, Green Bean, Beet and Chili Drink

~

Burns and wounds need concentrated vitamins and minerals to speed up cell repair and replacement. The chili will help to reduce any pain; orange provides vitamin C, folate and bioflavonoids; green beans supply phosphorus to help cell formation; and beet provides carotenes.

~

*Makes about 1 cup*
*(8 fl oz/250 ml); serves 1*

~

*1 small (serrano) chili*
*3 oz (90 g) green beans*
½ *medium beet (beetroot), chopped*
*1 orange, peeled (retaining some white pith)*
*and chopped*

In a juice extractor, process first the chili, then the beans, beet and orange.

## Parsley and Orange Healer

~

After surgery, it is a good idea to have foods that provide lots of vitamin C to boost the immune function, as well as folate for new cell growth and repair, and iron for healthy red blood cells and oxygen transport. The vitamin C in orange juice encourages better absorption of iron from greens.

~

*Makes about 1 cup*
*(8 fl oz/250 ml); serves 1*

~

*1 oz (30 g) fresh parsley sprigs*
*3 oz (90 g) fresh spinach*
*1½ medium oranges, peeled*
*and chopped*

In a juice extractor, process first the parsley, then the spinach and oranges.

## Green Spinach and Pear Juice

~

This immune- and strength-building drink is good during convalescence, when you don't feel like eating a lot. You may want to dilute it a little with pure water. It contains vitamin C, carotenes, folate, iron and soluble fiber.

~

*Makes about 1¼ cups*
*(10 fl oz/310 ml); serves 1*

~

½ *oz (15 g) fresh parsley sprigs*
*2 oz (60 g) fresh spinach*
*1 pear, chopped*
½ *green bell pepper (capsicum), chopped*
*1 medium carrot, peeled and chopped*

In a juice extractor, process first the parsley, then the spinach, pear, pepper and carrot.

*Super Orange Booster*

# Detoxing & Cleansing

The benefits of a detoxification or internal cleansing program are numerous, even though it may require some restrictions on your diet for a short time. It allows your body to rid itself of toxins that have accumulated in many forms: preservatives, colorings and other additives to our foods; heavy metals and chemicals we've been exposed to at work or home; allergens from environmental or food sources; and drugs both medicinal and recreational. A cleansing, program may last 1–2 weeks only while a detoxing program may last 6–12 weeks. Both may include the following guidelines:

- Omit gluten-containing grains: wheat, rye, barley and oats
- Omit sugar and sugar-containing foods
- Omit dairy products except natural acidophilus yogurt
- Eat low-fat foods—no deep-fried foods or fatty snacks
- Omit caffeine: coffee, tea, chocolate, cola
- Omit alcohol
- Eat organic fruit, vegetables, lamb and chicken; don't eat beef, veal or pork
- Drink at least 6 glasses of pure water a day
- Eat fish 3 times a week (but not shellfish)
- Eat plenty of fresh fruit and vegetables, both raw and cooked, each day
- Eat plenty of brassica-family vegetables, such as broccoli, cabbage, cauliflower, Brussels sprouts and kohlrabi (these assist with detox)
- Eat plenty of rice and rice products and potatoes for carbohydrate intake

Some herbal teas increase liver function; dandelion tea is especially good for this. A soluble-fiber supplement, such as psyllium husks, mixed into drinks also helps to absorb toxins and assist in their elimination.

If you intend to follow a detox program for more than a few days, we advise you seek professional advice from a qualified nutrition consultant, herbalist or naturopath to assist you through the process and to monitor your health.

*Dandelion, Artichoke, Apple and Beet Detox Drink (see page 40)*

## Warm Grapefruit Drink

~

This old but effective remedy should be drunk on an empty stomach first thing in the morning. The bitter citrus juice promotes gallbladder function, which in turn helps stimulate the digestive system and prevents constipation.

~

*Makes about 1¼ cups*
*(10 fl oz/310 ml) grapefruit drink, or ¾ cup*
*(6 fl oz/180 ml) lemon drink; serves 1*

~

*1 grapefruit or lemon*
*½ cup (4 fl oz/125 ml) hot water*

Squeeze the juice from the grapefruit using a citrus juicer, or peel and chop the grapefruit into small pieces and process in a juice extractor. Pour into a cup and whisk in the hot water. Drink while warm.

## Apple, Pear and Beet Juice

~

For a spring cleaning any time of the year, one day a week eat only light foods such as vegetables, rice and fruit, and drink cleansing juices. The beet increases liver activity, while the psyllium absorbs any toxins released and aids in their elimination.

~

*Makes about 1¼ cups*
*(10 fl oz/310 ml); serves 1*

~

*1 medium apple, chopped*
*1 medium pear, chopped*
*½ large beet (beetroot), chopped*
*2 teaspoons psyllium husks*

In a juice extractor, process the apple, pear and beet. Whisk in psyllium and drink immediately.

## Orange and Apricot Whip

~

If you have given up smoking, drink this regularly to encourage the repair of lung tissue. The beta-carotene in the apricots is converted to vitamin A and helps in the maintenance of mucous membranes; an antioxidant. It also absorbs free radicals. Vitamin C and E (from the orange and wheat germ oil respectively), also antioxidants, are often depleted in those who smoke.

~

*Makes about 1⅓ cups*
*(11 fl oz/330 ml); serves 1–2*

~

*4½ oz (140 g) canned apricots in natural juice*
*¾ cup (6 fl oz/180 ml) fresh orange juice*
*1 teaspoon grated fresh ginger*
*½ teaspoon wheat germ oil*

In a blender, combine all the ingredients and blend until smooth.

## Low-allergy Sprout Juice

~

This mildly cleansing juice is made with foods that rarely contribute to allergies. Alfalfa contains vitamin C and chlorophyll and is a blood tonic that helps with internal cleansing. Celery is a natural diuretic that helps to flush toxins from the body.

~

*Makes about 1 cup*
*(8 fl oz/250 ml); serves 1*

~

*1 oz (30 g) alfalfa sprouts*
*1 apple, chopped*
*1½ celery stalks with leaves, chopped*

In a juice extractor, process first the alfalfa sprouts, then the apple and celery.

*Warm Grapefruit Drink*

## Cucumber and Beet Cocktail

~

Beet is used often for cleansing and to relieve constipation. Because it can have quite a strong effect on the body, we have diluted it with cucumber, an excellent cleanser, and soda water.

~

*Makes about 2 cups*
*(16 fl oz/500 ml); serves 2*

~

½ medium beet (beetroot), chopped
1 small cucumber, chopped
1½ cups (12 fl oz/375 ml) soda water
squeeze of fresh lime juice

In a juice extractor, process beet, then the cucumber. Add the soda water and lime juice and stir well.

## Cucumber, Celery and Rosemary Juice

~

For those with recurrent thrush or candida, this juice helps to reduce infection and restore a healthy digestion. The celery and cucumber cleanse, the garlic and rosemary are antibacterial agents, and the psyllium helps absorb and remove toxins. If you cannot tolerate fresh garlic, use one or two strong garlic capsules.

~

*Makes about 1 cup*
*(8 fl oz/250 ml); serves 1*

~

½-inch (1.25-cm) piece fresh ginger
1 clove garlic (optional)
1 small cucumber, chopped
1 celery stalk with leaves, chopped
1 teaspoon finely chopped fresh rosemary
1 teaspoon psyllium husks or pectin

In a juice extractor, process the ginger, garlic, cucumber and celery. Whisk in the rosemary and psyllium or pectin.

## Apple, Spinach & Onion Juice

~

People working with mercury, lead or other heavy metals may benefit from a regular serve of this brisk brew. Spinach contains glutathione, which aids detoxification. Onion and garlic are high in sulphur compounds, which help combat heavy metal buildup. Psyllium helps absorb and eliminate toxins.

~

*Makes about ¾ cup*
*(6 fl oz/180 ml); serves 1*

~

2 small apples, chopped
¼ small red (Spanish) onion, chopped
2 oz (60 g) fresh spinach leaves
1 clove garlic
1½ teaspoons psyllium husks

In a juice extractor, process the apples, onion, spinach and garlic, then whisk in the psyllium.

## Artichoke, Orange and Carrot Juice

~

This is excellent if you have eaten foods with additives, such as colorings and preservatives. Artichokes possess choleretic qualities, which increase bile to help detoxification. Carrots and oranges have antioxidants and psyllium helps absorb and eliminate toxins.

~

*Makes about 1¼ cups*
*(10 fl oz/310 ml); serves 1*

~

½ small artichoke, tough outer leaves removed
1 orange, peeled
2 medium carrots, chopped
2 teaspoons psyllium husks

Trim and discard ends of artichoke's centre leaves. Cut artichoke into small pieces. In a juice extractor, process ingredients before whisking in psyllium.

*Cucumber and Beet Cocktail*

## Orange, Red Pepper and Turmeric Detoxifier

~

Some people are exposed to all kinds of chemicals in their daily working life. These can be absorbed through the skin and lungs and cause stress on the body. This drink assists the body to detoxify any accumulation of chemical toxins. Turmeric has liver-protective qualities, and the dandelion helps to improve the functional capacity of the liver. Psyllium absorbs any toxins released and helps to eliminate them from the body, while the orange juice and pepper provide vitamin C and carotenes, antioxidants that reduce free-radical activity.

~

*Makes about 1¼ cups*
*(10 fl oz/310 ml); serves 1*

~

*1 teaspoon dried roasted dandelion root*
*¼ cup (2 fl oz/60 ml) boiling water*
*1 orange, peeled and chopped*
*½ large red bell pepper (capsicum), seeded and chopped*
*1¼-inch (3-cm) piece fresh turmeric*
*2 teaspoons psyllium husks*

In a large mug, combine the dandelion root and boiling water. Cover and let steep for 10 minutes. Strain, reserving liquid. Let it cool. In a juice extractor, process orange, bell pepper and turmeric. Add to the dandelion tea, whisk in the psyllium, and drink immediately.

## Dandelion, Artichoke, Apple and Beet Detox Drink

~

This drink provides several nutrients and herbs that promote liver and gallbladder function. Dandelion root enhances bile flow, while beet contains beta-carotene, an important source of antioxidants. Psyllium is a soluble fiber that absorbs waste matter and encourages its elimination from the body.

~

*Makes about 1¼ cups*
*(10 fl oz/310 ml); serves 1*

~

*2 teaspoons dried roasted dandelion root*
*¼ cup (2 fl oz/60 ml) boiling water*
*¼ small artichoke*
*½ small beet (beetroot), chopped*
*2 apples, chopped*
*1½ teaspoons psyllium husks*

Put the dandelion root in a cup and add the water. Let steep for 10 minutes. Strain and set the liquid aside to cool. Remove the tough outer leaves from the artichoke and trim the ends of the remaining centre leaves. Cut the artichoke into small pieces. In a juice extractor, process the artichokes, beet and apples. Combine with the dandelion tea and then whisk in the psyllium husks. Drink immediately.

## Clean Green Juice

~

This bright green drink contains juices rich in chlorophyll, an excellent body cleanser, as well as such nutrients as folate, carotene and potassium, all essential for good health.

~

*Makes about 1 cup*
*(8 fl oz/250 ml); serves 1*

~

*5 small spinach leaves*
*1 medium green bell pepper (capsicum), chopped*
*1 celery stalk with leaves, chopped*
*2 large lettuce leaves*

In a juice extractor, process the spinach, then the pepper, celery and lettuce.

*Clean Green Juice*

# Weighing Up

Some people have trouble reducing weight while others, who are underweight, find it difficult to put on weight. And then there are those with eating disorders, a lack of appetite, or with body-building needs.

The drinks in this chapter are designed to assist in several areas, but are not intended as a solution to weight problems. For example, we have included several drinks to aid weight reduction and appetite suppression. Real weight loss, however, is the result of a healthy diet and an exercise program.

Each person is unique and requires a specific eating program and calorie (kilojoule) intake, depending on his or her level of activity, height and body type, and overall health. If you wish to lose or gain weight, a nutrition consultant can help you learn how to do so while improving your health at the same time. For instance, eating fatty foods is not the best choice for those wishing to add pounds, as it will only create other health problems in the long run. Instead, a diet rich in good-quality carbohydrates and protein, along with "good" fats, is needed.

Radical weight-loss diets that restrict all but a few foods are to be avoided at all costs. You run the risk of becoming deficient in essential nutrients with this type of diet. And skipping meals regularly to reduce weight has the opposite effect—where you may feel 'light', your body slows its metabolism a little to compensate for the reduced energy supply. Eating regular healthy meals is the main aim.

All the drinks in this chapter are delicious and can be served to anyone, not just those wanting to increase or decrease their weight.

*Lime and Strawberry Soda* (left; *see* page 44)
*Apricot and Cherimoya Whip* (right; *see* page 48)

### Lime and Strawberry Soda

~

This is a great drink to have when cutting your food intake, as it is light and delicious. It contains vitamin C and satisfies the urge for a special drink at any time.

~

*Makes about 1 cup*
*(8 fl oz/250 ml); serves 1*

~

*4 oz (125 g) fresh strawberries,*
*hulled, or thawed frozen*
*strawberries*
*½ lime, chopped*
*½ cup (4 fl oz/125 ml) soda water*

In a juice extractor, process the strawberries, then the lime. Add the soda water and stir to combine.

### Cucumber, Celery and Beet Juice

~

When trying to lose weight, drink juices that are high in nutrients but low in calories (kilojoules). As an added bonus, high-nutrient drinks such as this one also help to reduce feelings of tiredness and to boost immune function.

~

*Makes about 1¼ cups*
*(10 fl oz/310 ml); serves 1*

~

*1 small cucumber*
*2 celery stalks with leaves*
*1 medium tomato*
*½ small beet (beetroot)*
*½ apple*

Chop all the vegetables and fruit into small pieces and process in a juice extractor. Mix well.

### Peach and Mango Low-fat Shake

~

This is an excellent appetite suppressant for those wishing to lose weight, as the psyllium provides bulk in the intestines and promotes a feeling of fullness. Glycerine, which should be purchased from a pharmacy (chemist), also acts as an appetite suppressant.

~

*Makes about 1¼ cups*
*(10 fl oz/310 ml); serves 1*

~

*¾ cup (6 fl oz/180 ml) nonfat milk*
*or low-fat fortified soy milk, chilled*
*4½ oz (140 g) canned mixed peach*
*and mango in natural*
*juice, chilled*
*2 teaspoons psyllium husks*
*1–2 teaspoons glycerine*

In a blender, combine all the ingredients and blend until smooth.

*Cucumber, Celery and Beet Juice*

## Pineapple and Cucumber Juice

~

If you are on a weight-reduction diet, try this natural appetite suppressant. The enzyme in pineapple helps to inhibit the appetite and it teams well with the cucumber, which is filling and low in calories (kilojoules). The psyllium provides bulk, creating a feeling of fullness and helping to prevent constipation, a complaint that can arise in weight-loss programs.

~

*Makes about 1 cup*
*(8 fl oz/250 ml); serves 1*

~

*½ medium pineapple, peeled,*
*cored, and chopped*
*½ small cucumber, peeled*
*and chopped*
*2 teaspoons psyllium husks*

In a juice extractor, process the pineapple and cucumber and mix well. Whisk in the psyllium and drink immediately.

## Apple, Chili, Spinach and Celery Juice

~

Spirulina helps to reduce hunger, and celery is a natural diuretic that helps to prevent fluid retention. Chilies can help to increase the metabolic rate, while spinach contains chlorophyll, an excellent internal cleanser. Slippery elm or psyllium helps to produce a feeling of fullness.

~

*Makes about 1 cup*
*(8 fl oz/250 ml); serves 1*

~

*1 small serrano chili*
*2 oz (60 g) fresh spinach*
*1 celery stalk with leaves, chopped*
*1 apple, chopped*
*½ teaspoon spirulina*
*1 teaspoon slippery elm or*
*psyllium husks*

In a juice extractor, process first the chili, then the spinach, celery and apple. Whisk in the spirulina and slippery elm.

## Grape and Celery Juice

~

A light drink to boost the appetite. Parsley contains zinc, and green grapes and celery provide potassium. A deficiency of either of these minerals can contribute to poor appetite.

~

*Makes about ¾ cup*
*(6 fl oz/180 ml); serves 1*

~

*½ oz (15 g) fresh parsley sprigs*
*6 oz (185 g) green seedless grapes*
*1 celery stalk with leaves, chopped*

In a juice extractor, process the parsley, then the grapes and celery.

*Pineapple and Cucumber Juice*

## Pear Juice Body Balancer

~

A sports drink to have when you're weight-training or doing any heavy exercise. It contains the correct proportion of sugar and sodium to help balance your body's electrolytes.

~

*Makes about 1 cup*
*(8 oz/250 ml); serves 1*

~

*½ pear, chopped*
*½ cup (4 fl oz/125 ml) water*
*¼ teaspoon salt*

In a juice extractor, process the pear. Whisk in the water and salt.

## Apple Builder

~

This is a good drink for body builders. The dried apples contain carbohydrates for energy, while the nuts provide potassium, needed for energy release; magnesium for improved muscle tone and the prevention of muscle cramps; and calcium, needed for muscle movement. Milk and soy milk, of course, supply calcium and protein, and the egg supplies good-quality protein and iron, both essential for building muscles.

~

*Makes about 1¼ cups*
*(10 fl oz/310 ml); serves 1*

~

*5 dried apples*
*¼ cup (2 fl oz/60 ml) hot water*
*1 cup (8 fl oz/250 ml) milk or fortified soy milk*
*4 Brazil nuts*
*1 egg*
*2 teaspoons wheat germ*
*¼ teaspoon vanilla extract (essence)*

In a small bowl, soak apple in hot water for 15 minutes or until soft; drain. In a blender, combine apple and liquid and remaining ingredients and blend until smooth.

## Pink Plum Shake

~

If you have trouble putting on weight, this is the ideal drink. It provides carbohydrate, protein, iron, vitamin E, folate and a little zinc. Use fresh plums when they're in season, and drained canned plums at other times. The plums provide flavonoids, which help in the support structure, such as the connective tissue of the body.

~

*Makes about 1½ cups*
*(12 fl oz/375 ml); serves 1*

~

*3 small dark plums, halved and pitted*
*7 fl oz (200 ml) milk or soy milk*
*1 egg*
*1 teaspoon wheat germ*

In a blender, combine all the ingredients and blend until smooth.

## Apricot and Cherimoya Whip

~

To gain weight, don't eat poor-quality foods high in saturated fat. Choose highly nutritious foods with lots of carbohydrates, such as this drink, along with good-quality protein. Ingest essential fatty acids by eating nuts, seeds and fish. If cherimoya is unavailable, substitute with bananas.

~

*Makes about 1¼ cups*
*(10 fl oz/310 ml); serves 1*

~

*7 oz (200 g) cherimoya (custard apple), seeded*
*4½ oz (140 g) canned apricots in natural juice*
*½ cup (4 fl oz/125 ml) fresh orange juice*
*3 teaspoons fresh lime juice*

Scoop the cherimoya flesh into a blender and discard skin. Add the remaining ingredients and blend until smooth.

*Pink Plum Shake*

# Strawberry and Pumpkin Seed Health Shake

~

People recovering from any condition that causes undernutrition, such as anorexia nervosa, are often deficient in vital nutrients. This drink supplies many of those nutrients, such as zinc, provided by the pumpkin and sunflower seeds; vitamin C from the strawberries; B vitamins from the brewer's yeast; and carbohydrate and protein from the soy milk or milk. Tryptophan, a precursor of serotonin, the mood-enhancing hormone, is a bonus provided by the soy milk or milk and the pumpkin seeds.

~

*Makes about 1 cup*
*(8 fl oz/250 ml); serves 1*

~

*½ cup (4 fl oz/125 ml) low-fat milk*
*or fortified soy milk, chilled*
*4 oz (125 g) fresh strawberries,*
*hulled, or thawed frozen*
*strawberries*
*1 tablespoon pumpkin seed kernels*
*(pepitas), ground or very finely*
*chopped*
*2 teaspoons honey*
*¼–½ teaspoon brewer's*
*yeast, to taste*

In a blender, combine all the ingredients and blend until smooth. Serve immediately.

# Grapefruit, Carrot and Celery Juice

~

This is a drink packed with potassium, vitamin C and beta-carotene, all nutrients that are beneficial for those suffering from bulimia nervosa. In particular, the potassium helps to balance the body's electrolytes, which are disturbed as a result of this condition.

~

*Makes about 1¼ cups*
*(10 fl oz/310 ml); serves 1*

~

*½ large grapefruit, peeled*
*2 small carrots*
*1 celery stalk with leaves*

Chop all the ingredients into small pieces and process in a juice extractor. Mix well.

# Mango and Banana Whip

~

A smooth and tasty drink that contains beta-carotene, potassium, soluble fiber, essential fatty acids and zinc. It tastes so good, it helps to improve a poor appetite. If fresh mango is unavailable, substitute with frozen or canned mango in natural juice.

~

*Makes about 1½ cups*
*(12 fl oz/375 ml); serves 1–2*

~

*½ mango, peeled, cut from the pit,*
*and chopped*
*1 banana, peeled and chopped*
*¾ cup (6 fl oz/180 ml)*
*apple juice*
*1 tablespoon pumpkin seed kernels*
*(pepitas)*

In a blender, combine all the ingredients and blend until smooth. Add more apple juice if the drink appears too thick.

*Mango and Banana Whip*

# For Women Only

Women have special nutritional needs at different stages of life. The onset of menstruation, for example, can bring on premenstrual syndrome. This chapter includes several drinks to help alleviate the symptoms of PMS, which include cramping, depression, anxiety, food cravings and fluid retention.

Certain vitamins and minerals are important to women both before and after pregnancy. Before conception, it is essential to have enough folate in the diet to help prevent neural tube defects in the future fetus. Both mothers and their babies need extra nutrients during pregnancy, after delivery and while breastfeeding.

Such problems as infections, including cystitis and thrush, and cosmetic concerns such as cellulite may also be alleviated by proper nutrition.

Lately, there has been much talk about menopause and the best way to treat the associated symptoms. Research has been undertaken to study the effects of the phytoestrogens found in soy products and flaxseed (linseed). Many advances have been made in treating menopause naturally, and our drinks are designed to assist in reducing symptoms and enhancing the health.

*Fennel, Pineapple, Spinach and Ginger Juice*
(*see* page 54)

## Fennel, Pineapple, Spinach and Ginger Juice

~

To help relieve menstrual pain drink this juice daily for several days prior to and during the first few days of your period. Pineapple and ginger contain natural anti-inflammatory agents. Spinach provides magnesium, which helps reduce muscle cramping. Fennel soothes the digestive system.

~

*Makes about 1½ cups*
*(12 fl oz/375 ml); serves 1*

~

*½ medium pineapple, cored, peeled and chopped,*
*¼ large fennel bulb, chopped*
*2½ oz (75 g) fresh spinach*
*½-inch (1.25-cm) piece fresh ginger*

Mix well all the ingredients in a juice extractor.

## Grape and Dandelion Drink

~

Sometimes sugar cravings and fluid retention is caused by PMS. Dandelion is a natural diuretic. Grapes and brewer's yeast contain chromium, which helps balance blood sugar levels and reduce cravings. Brewer's yeast also contains vitamin B6, used to reduce fluid retention. Wheat germ oil provides vitamin E to help to reduce breast tenderness.

~

*Makes about 1 cup*
*(8 fl oz/250 ml); serves 1*

~

*1 dandelion leaf tea bag*
*¼ cup (2 fl oz/60 ml) boiling water*
*9 oz (280 g) red grapes*
*¼ teaspoon brewer's yeast*
*½ teaspoon wheat germ oil*

Put tea bag in a large mug and add boiling water. Cover and steep 10 minutes. Remove bag and let tea cool. In a juice extractor, process grapes, add to tea. Whisk in brewer's yeast and wheat germ oil.

## Orange and Spinach Juice

~

Depression can be another sympton of PMS. Folate is often lower in the body when depressed, so the orange and spinach will help replenish it. Spinach also has vitamin B6, which helps break down estrogen in the liver and reduces fluid retention.

~

*Makes about 1¼ cups*
*(10 fl oz/310 ml); serves 1*

~

*2 large oranges, peeled and chopped*
*3½ oz, (105 g) fresh spinach*
*½-inch (1.2-cm) piece fresh ginger*
*leaves from 1–2 sprigs fresh rosemary, chopped*

Process all the ingredients in a juice extractor.

## Chamomile and Peach Shake

~

This drink helps reduce any anxiety and nervousness that accompanies PMS. Soy milk and flaxseed contain phytoestrogens to help balance your own estrogen. Chamomile is a calming herb. Cinnamon and ginger help lift the spirits. Brewer's yeast contains B vitamins and chromium, to help balance blood sugar levels.

~

*Makes about 1¼ cups*
*(10 fl oz/310 ml); serves 1*

~

*1 chamomile tea bag*
*⅓ cup (3 fl oz/80 ml) boiling water*
*⅔ cup (5 fl oz/160 ml) low-fat fortified soy milk, chilled*
*5½ oz (165 g) canned peach slices, chilled and drained*
*1 tablespoon flaxseed (linseed), ground*
*1 teaspoon honey or sugar*
*½ teaspoon brewer's yeast*
*¼ teaspoon ground ginger*
*¼ teaspoon ground cinnamon*

Put tea bag in a cup, add boiling water. Cover, let steep 10 minutes. Remove bag, let tea cool. In a blender, combine tea and all ingredients. Blend.

*Orange and Spinach Juice*

## Fennel and Apricot Shake

~

A great drink for when breastfeeding. Fennel helps to calm upset stomachs and frazzled nerves. Milk or soy milk provides calcium. Almonds supply calcium and essential fatty acids. Apricots are a good source of beta-carotene.

~

*Makes about 1¾ cups
(14 fl oz/430 ml); serves 2*

~

*1 fennel tea bag
¼ cup (2 fl oz/60 ml) boiling water
¾ cup (6 fl oz/185 ml) milk or fortified soy milk
5 drained canned apricot halves
2 teaspoons ground almonds
1 teaspoon honey*

Place tea bag in a cup and add boiling water. Let steep 15 minutes. Remove bag and chill tea. In a blender, combine tea and all ingredients; blend.

## Apricot & Raspberry Smoothie

~

This smoothie supplies calcium, protein, vitamins C, B, D, E, K, zinc, iron, folate and bioflavonoids; all essential for the good health of both mother and baby during pregnancy.

~

*Makes about 1½ cups
(12 fl oz/375 ml); serves 1–2*

~

*50g dried apricots, chopped
½ cup (4 fl oz/125 ml) water
½ cup (4 fl oz/125 ml) low-fat milk or fortified soy milk
1 tablespoon tahini
75 g fresh or thawed frozen raspberries
1 teaspoon honey, or to taste*

In a small saucepan, combine apricots and water. Bring to boil, reduce heat, cover and cook for 15 minutes. Let cool. In a blender, combine apricots and liquid with remaining ingredients and blend.

## Grape and Raspberry Drink

~

After giving birth, it may assist to have nutrients that promote the tone and strength of the pelvic tissues. Raspberry leaf tea has been used for this purpose for many years. Grapes are thought to help with breast milk production, and ginger and cinnamon reduce weakness and tiredness and are mood enhancers.

~

*Makes about 1 cup
(8 fl oz/250 ml); serves 1*

~

*1 raspberry leaf tea bag
⅓ cup (3 fl oz/80 ml) boiling water
7 oz (210 g) grapes
¾-inch (2-cm) piece fresh ginger
¼ teaspoon ground cinnamon*

Put tea bag in a large mug and add boiling water. Cover, let steep 15 minutes. Remove bag and let tea cool. In a juice extractor, process grapes and ginger. Add to tea along with cinnamon and mix well.

## Spinach and Pear Juice

~

If you are planning on starting a family, drink this juice every day for a couple of months before conception and during the first 12 weeks of pregnancy. It will boost your folate supplies, needed to help reduce neural tube defects in the developing fetus. The pear fiber helps reduce constipation, a common complaint during pregnancy.

~

*Makes about 1¼ cups
(10 fl oz/310 ml); serves 1*

~

*3 oz (90 g) chopped broccoli
1 pear, chopped
2 oz (60 g) fresh spinach
1 oz (30 g) watercress*

In a juice extractor, process first the broccoli, then the spinach, watercress and pear.

*Apricot & Raspberry Smoothie*

# Cooling Orange and Sage Drink

~

Sage is an herb that has been shown to reduce hot flashes during menopause. The vitamin C and bioflavonoids in the orange help to strengthen blood capillary walls and to reduce the dilation that increases the severity of hot flashes. If you cannot find fresh sage, use dried sage leaves or a sage tea bag.

~

*Makes about ¾ cup*
*(6 fl oz/180 ml); serves 1*

~

*15 fresh sage leaves or 7 dried sage leaves, crumbled*
*½ cup (4 fl oz/125 ml) boiling water*
*1 teaspoon grated orange zest*
*⅓ cup (3 fl oz/80 ml) fresh orange juice*
*½ teaspoon honey*

Put the sage leaves into a small bowl and add the boiling water. Let steep for 10 minutes. Let cool to room temperature. Strain the liquid into a serving cup and whisk in the orange zest, juice and honey.

# Silky Mango Whip

~

Menopausal symptoms can be alleviated to some extent with natural foods. Red clover, flaxseed (linseed) and tofu contain phytoestrogens that help to balance estrogen levels, thus reducing hot flashes and vaginal dryness. Mango supplies beta-carotene and vitamin C.

~

*Makes about 1¼ cups*
*(10 fl oz/310 ml); serves 1–2*

~

*1 tablespoon dried red clover*
*¼ cup (2 fl oz/60 ml) boiling water*
*1 tablespoon flaxseed (linseed)*
*5 oz (155 g) silken tofu*
*1 medium mango, peeled, cut from the pit and chopped, or 110 g frozen or canned mango*
*½ cup (4 fl oz/125 ml) apple juice*

In a cup, combine the red clover and boiling water. Let steep for 15 minutes. Strain, reserving the liquid. Grind the flaxseed in a coffee grinder until fine. Add the red clover tea and all the remaining ingredients and blend until smooth.

# Stress Soother

~

If you are suffering stress and anxiety due to menopause, this drink can help to calm you down. Valerian is a calming herb, while rosemary is an uplifting herb. Celery and apple are cooling for the body and help to relieve hot flashes.

~

*Makes 1¼ cups*
*(10 fl oz/310 ml); serves 1*

~

*1 valerian tea bag*
*1 teaspoon chopped fresh rosemary*
*¼ cup (2 fl oz/60 ml) boiling water*
*1 apple, chopped*
*1 celery stalk with leaves, chopped*
*1 teaspoon honey or sugar, to taste*

Put the tea bag and rosemary in a cup and add the water. Let steep for 15 minutes. Strain, reserving the liquid. In a juice extractor, process the apple and celery. Whisk in the valerian tea and honey or sugar.

*Cooling Orange and Sage Drink* (left)
*Stress Soother* (right)

## Orange and Beet Juice with Fenugreek

~

While there is not a great deal that can be done about cellulite, increasing waste-matter excretion from the body via the lymphatic system may help. Fenugreek is an excellent lymphatic herb and beet and celery help improve elimination.

~

*Makes about 1¼ cups*
*(10 fl oz/310 ml); serves 1*

~

*2 teaspoons fenugreek*
*¼ cup (2 fl oz/60 ml) hot water*
*1 medium beet (beetroot), chopped*
*1 celery stalk with leaves, chopped*
*1 orange, peeled and chopped*

Put fenugreek in a large mug. Add hot water, let steep 10 minutes. Strain, reserving liquid, cool to room temperature. In a juice extractor, process beet, then celery and orange. Add to liquid and whisk.

## Bell Pepper & Cucumber Juice

~

For the relief of thrush, acidophilus helps reestablish healthy bowel flora, and psyllium absorbs toxins from unfriendly bacteria. A garlic capsule, taken 2 hours before or after this drink, will also help. (Don't take garlic at the same time as it is an antibiotic and will kill off good bacteria in the acidophilus.)

~

*Makes about 1 cup*
*(8 fl oz/250 ml); serves 1*

~

*½ small green bell pepper (capsicum), chopped*
*1 medium unpeeled cucumber, scrubbed and chopped*
*1 celery stalk with leaves, chopped*
*½ teaspoon acidophilus powder*
*1 teaspoon psyllium husks*

In a juice extractor, process pepper, then cucumber and celery. Whisk in acidophilus and psyllium.

## Dandelion, Carrot and Orange Drink

~

For those who are prone to benign breast lumps, this drink contains dandelion root, which improves liver function. The carrots supply beta-carotene to help reduce symptoms. Vitamin E from wheat germ oil is also important to help reduce symptoms and psyllium helps improve bowel function. Women with chronic constipation seem more prone to benign breast lumps.

~

*Makes about 1 cup*
*(8 fl oz/250 ml); serves 1*

~

*2 teaspoons dried roasted dandelion root*
*1 teaspoon honey*
*⅓ cup (3 fl oz/80 ml) boiling water*
*2 medium carrots, chopped*
*1 teaspoon psyllium husks*
*1 teaspoon finely grated orange zest*
*½ teaspoon wheat germ oil*

Put dandelion root and honey in a cup, add boiling water and mix well. Cover, let steep for 10 minutes. Strain and let cool. In a juice extractor, process the carrots. In a glass, combine tea and carrot juice. Whisk in psyllium, orange zest and wheat germ oil.

## Watermelon Juice

~

Watermelon has high water content, is a wonderful diuretic and is useful for soothing cystitis and other urinary tract infections.

~

*Makes about 2 cups*
*(16 fl oz/500ml); serves 2*

~

*2½-lb (1.25-kg) piece watermelon, chilled, seeded, and chopped.*

Process the watermelon in a juice extractor.

*Watermelon Juice*

# Family Tonics

Fresh juices and fruit drinks are beneficial for all members of the family, from the very young to the very old. Particular nutrients are important at different ages, such as calcium for growing children and antioxidants for adults and fiber for the elderly.

This chapter includes after-school drinks for children, who usually come home from school ravenous and looking for snacks. We also suggest that you keep healthy foods on hand, like nuts, wholesome cookies, bread and tasty spreads, cereals, milk or soy milk and fresh fruit.

For teenagers, who are often concerned with their skin and weight, we offer a cleansing juice to promote healthy skin, as well as a delicious low-fat chocolate-banana shake. You will also find bone-building drinks good for all children and teens.

Cardiovascular health and aging are important issues for adults, and certain nutrients help to promote and maintain heart health and to decrease the effects of aging. Antioxidants play a large role here, for they help to get rid of free radicals and reduce their damaging effects on the body.

You will also find calming and stress-reducing drinks for those with busy lives, and drinks designed to make sure that vegetarians are receiving all the nutrients they need. Finally, a breakfast smoothie, an after-work digestion-improving cocktail, general juices for kids, and a family fruit juice are featured.

*Persimmon or Mango*
*Family Breakfast Drink*
(*see* page 72)

### Fennel Tummy Soother

~

A soothing drink for babies. Fennel is a carminative herb that helps reduce wind and colic in the digestive system. You can dilute this drink further by adding extra cooled, boiled water, if you prefer.

~

*Makes about ½ cup*
*(4 fl oz/125 ml); serves 1*
*(depending on the age)*

~

*1 fennel tea bag*
*1 cup (8 fl oz/250 ml) boiling water*
*1½ oz (45 g) chopped fresh fennel (optional)*
*¼ cup (2 fl oz/60 ml) boiled water, cooled*

Put the tea bag in a cup and add the boiling water. Cover and let steep for 5 minutes. Remove the tea bag and let the tea cool. Process the fennel, if using, in a juice extractor. Combine 2 tablespoons of the fennel tea with the cooled boiled water and the fresh fennel juice, if using. Save the remaining fennel tea for another drink.

### Pear and Raspberry Juice

~

A pretty juice that children will happily drink. The pear provides fiber, along with carbohydrates for energy. The raspberries supply some beta-carotene, an essential nutrient. Water is added to make the juice easier for children to digest.

~

*Makes about 1 cup*
*(8 fl oz/250 ml); serves 1*

~

*4 oz (125 g) fresh or thawed frozen raspberries*
*½ pear, chopped*
*⅓ cup (3 fl oz/80 ml) water*

In a juice extractor, process the raspberries, then the pear. Add the water and mix well.

### Pear and Cucumber Juice

~

A light and delicious juice containing nutrients to promote bone growth in children and bone maintenance in adults. Cucumber contains some calcium and magnesium, both important for bones. Parsley contains some magnesium as well. The apple and pear provide some soluble fiber and carbohydrate for energy.

~

*Makes about 1¼ cups*
*(10 fl oz/310 oz); serves 1*

~

*½ medium pear, chopped*
*1 small cucumber, chopped*
*½ medium apple, chopped*
*1 oz (30 g) fresh parsley sprigs*

Process all the ingredients in a juice extractor.

*Pear and Raspberry Juice*

## Passion Fruit and Banana Shake

~

An after-school drink for kids that is packed with calcium, potassium and friendly bacteria for intestinal health. Its low glycemic index factor makes it a slow-release energy drink.

~

*Makes about 1½ cups (12 fl oz/375 ml); serves 1–2*

~

*1 medium passion fruit*
*1 medium banana, peeled and chopped*
*¾ cup (6 fl oz/180 ml) low-fat milk or fortified soy milk, chilled*
*¼ cup (2 oz/60 g) vanilla acidophilus yogurt*

Scoop out the passion fruit flesh and put in a blender. Add all the remaining ingredients and blend until smooth.

## Strawberry and Pineapple Whip

~

A drink high in vitamin C for kids to have after school or for breakfast. It contains enzymes that help with digestion and carbohydrates for energy, while strawberries promote clear skin.

~

*Makes about 2 cups (16 fl oz/500 ml); serves 2*

~

*4 oz (125 g) fresh strawberries, hulled, or thawed frozen strawberries*
*½ medium pear, chopped*
*¼ medium pineapple, peeled, cored and chopped*
*1 orange, peeled and chopped*

In a juice extractor, process first the strawberries, then the pear, pineapple and orange.

## Carrot and Apple Cider Cocktail

~

An aperitif to stimulate the digestive juices before dinner.

~

*Makes about 1¼ cups (10 fl oz/310 ml); serves 2*

~

*2 medium carrots, chilled and chopped*
*¾ cup (6 fl oz/180 ml) sparkling apple cider, chilled*
*1 teaspoon apple cider vinegar*
*2 teaspoons finely chopped fresh mint*
*ice cubes*

Process the carrots in a juice extractor. Combine the carrot juice with the cider, vinegar and mint. Pour over ice cubes in cocktail glasses.

*Carrot and Apple Cider Cocktail*

## Clear-skin Strawberry Juice

~

Teenagers take note: This juice helps to cleanse the skin from the inside and reduces pimple outbreaks. The strawberries provide vitamin C, and the cucumber is an excellent natural diuretic and internal cleanser.

~

*Makes about 1 cup
(8 fl oz/250 ml); serves 1*

~

*8 oz (250 g) fresh strawberries, hulled, or thawed frozen strawberries
1 small cucumber, chopped*

Process the strawberries and cucumber in a juice extractor.

## Chocolate–Banana Smoothie

~

This energy-boosting, low-fat filling drink for teenagers supplies carbohydrate, calcium, potassium and vitamin E. If making it for children under two years of age, use whole milk.

~

*Makes about 1¼ cups
(10 fl oz/310 ml); serves 1*

~

*1 medium sugar/lady finger banana, peeled and chopped
¾ cup (6 fl oz/180 ml) low-fat milk or fortified soy milk
1 teaspoon unsweetened cocoa powder
1 teaspoon wheat germ*

In a blender, combine all the ingredients and blend until smooth.

## Kiwi Fruit and Apple Juice

~

This is an all-round healthy drink for the whole family. It contains vitamin C, some soluble fiber from the pectin in the apples, and enzymes that aid digestion.

~

*Makes about 2½ cups
(20 fl oz/625 ml); serves 3–4*

~

*4 large kiwi fruit, chopped
4 large green apples, chopped*

Process all the ingredients in a juice extractor. Mix well.

*Clear-skin Strawberry Juice*

# Orange, Pepper and Alfalfa Juice

~

This juice provides nutrients that help to ensure heart health. Vitamin C, beta-carotene, potassium and chlorophyll are all-important heart and circulatory-system nutrients.

~

**Makes about 1 cup**
**(8 fl oz/250 ml); serves 1**

~

1 large orange, peeled and chopped
1 medium red bell pepper
(capsicum), chopped
2 oz (60g) alfalfa sprouts
4 fresh cilantro (fresh coriander)
sprigs with stems

Process all the ingredients in a juice extractor. Mix well.

# Calming Prune and Chamomile Drink

~

Try this when you need to relax. Chamomile is a calming herb, while prunes provide pantothenic acid (B5), essential for reducing stress. The bioflavonoids in the orange protect against free radicals, which are created when stress is high. Yogurt contains B vitamins, which are also important to help the nervous system to function well.

~

**Makes about 1⅓ cups**
**(11 fl oz/330 ml); serves 1**

~

1 chamomile tea bag, or 1 teaspoon
dried chamomile
¾ cup (6 fl oz/180 ml) boiling
water
½ cup (4 oz/125 g) natural
acidophilus yogurt
6 prunes, pitted
1 teaspoon grated orange zest
1 teaspoon honey

Put the tea bag or chamomile in a cup and add the boiling water. Let steep for 10 minutes. Strain, reserving the liquid, and chill the liquid. In a blender, combine the tea and all the remaining ingredients and blend until smooth.

# Chamomile, Mango and Strawberry Soother

~

If you need a calming drink after a stressful time, this drink can do wonders. Chamomile is a calming herb, and strawberries and mangoes are thought to be calming foods. Wheat germ provides essential B vitamins, which help you to cope with stress, and milk provides tryptophan, which aids in calming the mind. To prevent unnecessary anxiety, reduce the amount of caffeine and sugar you ingest.

~

**Makes about 1½ cups**
**(12 fl oz/375 ml); serves 1–2**

~

1 chamomile tea bag
¼ cup (2 fl oz/60 ml) boiling water
½ cup (4 fl oz/125 ml) cold low-fat
milk or fortified soy milk, chilled
3 oz (90 g) chopped mango
4 oz (125 g) fresh strawberries,
hulled, or thawed frozen
strawberries
2 teaspoons wheat germ

Put the chamomile tea bag in a cup and add the boiling water. Cover and let steep for 10 minutes. Remove the tea bag and let the tea cool. In a blender, combine the teas and all the remaining ingredients and blend until smooth.

*Orange, Pepper and Alfalfa Juice*

## Peppery Orange and Watercress Juice

~

Good for vegetarians or anyone wanting a boost in folate, iron, vitamin C and carotene.

~

*Makes 1¼ cups*
*(10 fl oz/310 ml); serves 1*

~

*2 oz (60 g) mushrooms, chopped*
*2 oz (60 g) watercress*
*1 oz (30 g) arugula (rocket)*
*2 oranges, peeled and chopped*
*1 lime, peeled and chopped*

In a juice extractor, process first the mushrooms, then the watercress, arugula, oranges and lime.

## Banana–Peanut Butter Shake

~

Vegetarians need another source of protein, vitamin B12 and iron—nutrients abundant in meat and poultry. This drink contains these and vitamin E, fiber, potassium, lecithin, B vitamins and calcium. The yolk is optional if you don't eat eggs.

~

*Makes about 1⅓ cups*
*(11 fl oz/330 ml); serves 1*

~

*¾ cup (6 fl oz/180 ml) fortified soy milk*
*1 tablespoon peanut butter*
*1 ripe medium banana, peeled*
*2 teaspoons wheat germ*
*¼ cup (2 oz/60 g) natural*
*acidophilus yogurt or soy yogurt*
*1 egg yolk (optional)*
*1 teaspoon brewer's yeast (optional if taste disliked)*
*Pinch ground nutmeg*

In a blender, combine all ingredients except nutmeg Blend then pour into glass and sprinkle with nutmeg.

## Orange, Carrot & Papaya Juice

~

If your children avoid eating vegetables, serve them this delicious juice. The carrots provide essential beta-carotene; the orange supplies vitamin C; and the papaya adds vitamin C, beta-carotene and enzymes that aid in digestion.

~

*Makes about 1 cup*
*(8 fl oz/250 ml); serves 1–2 (depending on age)*

~

*400 g papaya, peeled, seeded and chopped*
*1 orange, peeled and chopped*
*1 carrot, chopped*

Process the ingredients in a juice extractor. Mix well.

## Persimmon or Mango Family Breakfast Drink

~

This hearty drink supplies many essential nutrients. Persimmons and mangos are rich in beta-carotene, sunflower seeds are rich in essential fatty acids, and milk/soy milk and yogurt provide calcium. Wheat germ contributes fiber and vitamin E. For a year-round drink, use persimmon in winter and mango in summer.

~

*Makes about 3 cups*
*(24 fl oz/750 ml); serves 3–4*

~

*7 oz (210 g) chopped ripe persimmon or mango*
*1 cup (8 fl oz/250 ml) milk or fortified soy milk*
*½ cup (4 oz/125 g) natural*
*acidophilus yogurt*
*1 medium passion fruit, halved, pulp removed*
*3 teaspoons wheat germ*
*3 teaspoons sunflower seed kernels*
*⅓ cup (3 fl oz/80 ml) water*

In a blender, combine all the ingredients and blend until smooth. Add a little extra water if necessary to reach a drinkable consistency

*Orange, Carrot and Papaya Juice*

## Apple, Celery and Ginger Juice

~

This juice is an excellent cardiovascular and heart tonic. The celery is high in potassium, which helps to regulate blood pressure; and the apple contains pectin, which helps to reduce cholesterol levels. Ginger has many properties but is used here to add a flavor zing.

~

*Makes about 1¼ cups
(10 fl oz/310 ml); serves 1*

~

*2 Granny Smith or other tart green apples, chopped
2 celery stalks with leaves, chopped
¾-inch (2-cm) piece fresh ginger*

Process all the ingredients in a juice extractor. Mix well.

## Blueberry Bone Builder

~

Blueberries give this drink a delicious flavor and provide fiber and beta-carotene. The milk provides calcium, and the nuts provide magnesium and boron, all essential nutrients for bones. Vitamin D, synthesized in the body when exposed to sunlight, is also important. Remember too, that weight-bearing exercise is necessary to encourage bone-building, so walk regularly, and play tennis or squash or any other sport where you are on your feet and using your legs.

~

*Makes about 1⅓ cups
(11 fl oz/330 ml); serves 1*

~

*5 dried apricots, chopped
2 tablespoons hot water
1 cup (8 fl oz/250 ml) low-fat milk
or fortified soy milk
8 hazelnuts
4 oz (125 g) fresh or thawed frozen blueberries*

Put the dried apricots in a small bowl and add the hot water. Let soak for 15 minutes, or until soft. In a blender, combine the apricots and their liquid with all the remaining ingredients and blend until smooth.

## Pumpkin, Grapefruit and Parsley Juice

~

This juice could be called a liquid antioxidant, as it is high in beta-carotene and vitamin C, with a little selenium, all of which play vital roles in the body, helping to reduce the effects of aging and boost the immune system.

~

*Makes about 1¼ cups
(10 fl oz/310 ml); serves 1*

~

*4½ oz (140 g) pumpkin, chopped
1 grapefruit, peeled and chopped
2 fresh parsley sprigs with stems*

Process all the ingredients in a juice extractor. Mix well.

*Apple, Celery and Ginger Juice* (left)
*Blueberry Bone Builder* (right)

## Pear and Mango Shake

~

This is a nutritious drink for older people. It contains lots of soluble fiber to help prevent constipation. The wheat germ contributes vitamin E; the milk adds calcium; the yogurt supplies calcium, friendly bacteria, vitamin B12 and folate; and the mango provides beta-carotene, which helps prevent cataracts.

~

*Makes about 1½ cups
(12 fl oz/375 ml); serves 2*

~

*3 oz (90 g) chopped mango
¾ cup (6 fl oz/180 ml) low-fat milk
or fortified soy milk
1 teaspoon wheat germ
2 oz (60 g) natural acidophilus
yogurt
4½ oz (140 g) canned pears in
natural juice, drained
honey or sugar, to taste*

In a blender, combine all the ingredients and blend until smooth.

## Pear, Apple and Pineapple Juice

~

We recommend this juice for adults, especially the elderly, who may be prone to constipation and arthritis. The pear and apple provides excellent fiber to relieve constipation, while the pineapple contains bromelain, an enzyme that has been shown to reduce the inflammation of arthritis.

~

*Makes about 1¼ cups
(10 fl oz/310 ml); serves 1*

~

*½ medium pear, chopped
½ medium apple, chopped
½ medium pineapple, peeled, cored
and chopped*

Process all the ingredients in a juice extractor.

## Orange, Carrot, Guava and Corn Juice

~

This drink is packed with antioxidants, which are a natural form of anti-aging nutrients for adults.

~

*Makes about 1 cup
(8 fl oz/250 ml); serves 1*

~

*1 medium carrot
1 orange, zest grated, peel cut off
½ large guava
3 oz (90 g) fresh or thawed frozen
corn kernels*

Cut the carrot, orange and guava into small pieces. Process the carrot, orange, guava, and orange zest in a juice extractor and mix well.

*Pear and Mango Shake* (left)
*Pear, Apple and Pineapple Juice* (right)

# Juice Remedies

In this chapter you will find an A–Z listing of common health problems, along with drinks designed to assist with their treatment. Included are such conditions as acne, bronchitis, constipation, eczema, headaches, irritable bowel syndrome, sinusitis, sore throats, and wounds.

These drinks are not to be considered cures or sole treatments for any of these conditions. For any health concerns, we urge you to seek professional advice.

Some of the drinks in this chapter are medicinal in flavor because they include strong-tasting herbs such as dandelion root or sage that supply health-improving nutrition. In most cases, you may need to ingest the drinks on a regular basis in order to gain long-lasting benefits. This is because the nutrients have a preventative rather than a quick-fix effect.

As with most other drinks in this book, all the ones in this chapter can be taken either for a specific condition or to promote good health in general. For serious health problems, always seek the advice of a doctor.

*Cherry Juice* (*see* page 94)

## Carrot, Cucumber, Apple and Watercress Juice
### (Acne fighter)

~

This drink is an excellent detoxifier and internal cleanser.

~

*Makes about 1⅓ cups*
*(11 oz/330 g); serves 1*

~

*2 teaspoons roasted dandelion root*
*¼ cup (2 fl oz/60 ml) boiling water*
*1 oz (30 g) watercress*
*2 carrots, chopped*
*1 small cucumber, chopped*
*½ medium apple, chopped*

Put dandelion root in a mug, add boiling water and steep for 10 minutes. Strain, reserving liquid. In a juice extractor, process first watercress, then carrots, cucumber and apple. Whisk in dandelion liquid.

## Orange Blood Builder
### (Anemia preventer)

~

Anemia can be caused by lack of iron, folate or vitamin B12. This drink contains all three nutrients to help maintain healthy blood.

~

*Makes about 1 cup*
*(8 fl oz/250 ml); serves 1*

~

*5 dried apricots, finely chopped*
*½ cup (4 fl oz/125 ml) water*
*¾ cup (6 fl oz/180 ml) fresh orange juice*
*½ oz (15 g) chopped fresh parsley*
*½ teaspoon spirulina*

In a saucepan, combine apricots and water. Bring to boil, then reduce heat. Cover, cook for 15 minutes. Set aside to cool. In a blender, combine apricots and liquid and all ingredients. Blend until smooth.

## Cucumber, Apple, Turmeric and Ginger Juice
### (Arthritis reliever)

~

Turmeric and feverfew have anti-inflammatory qualities, and the cucumber and apple contain silica, needed for healthy bones and connective tissue. This drink will help reduce pain of arthritis.

~

*Makes about 1 cup*
*(8 fl oz/250 ml); serves 1*

~

*1 small cucumber, chopped*
*1 medium green apple, chopped*
*1-inch (2.5-cm) piece fresh turmeric*
*½-inch (1.2-cm) piece fresh ginger*
*5 fresh feverfew leaves, very finely chopped*

In a juice extractor, process cucumber, apple, turmeric and ginger. Whisk in feverfew.

## Pineapple, Celery, Ginger and Watercress Juice
### (Arthritis reliever)

~

An anti-inflammatory drink. The pineapple, ginger and celery all have anti-inflammatory properties, and the watercress provides some folate, chlorophyll and iron.

~

*Makes about 1¼ cups*
*(10 fl oz/310 ml); serves 1*

~

*1 teaspoon celery seeds, grounded (optional, if unavailable)*
*¼ large pineapple, peeled, cored, and chopped*
*2 celery stalks with leaves, chopped*
*2½ oz (75 g) watercress*
*½-inch (1.2-cm) piece fresh ginger*

In a juice extractor, process pineapple, celery, watercress and ginger. Whisk in celery seeds.

*Pineapple, Celery, Ginger and Watercress Juice* (right)
*Carrot and Parsley Juice* (left; see page 82)

## Carrot and Lime Juice
### (Asthma tonic)
~

Watercress contains magnesium, which helps relax airway muscles; ginger helps expel excess mucus; carrots provide beta-carotene for mucous membrane care; and limes provide vitamin C, which boosts the immune system and reduces inflammation.

~

*Makes about 1 cup
(8 fl oz/250 ml); serves 1*

~

*½ medium lime, peeled and chopped
1 oz (30 g) watercress
½-inch (1.2-cm) piece fresh ginger
3 medium carrots, chopped
1 teaspoon grated lime zest*

In a juice extractor, process lime, watercress, ginger and carrots. Whisk in the lime zest.

## Guava, Apple and Chili Juice
### (Back-pain easer)
~

The turmeric contains anti-inflammatory ingredients and the guava vitamin C. Chili helps by depleting substance P in sensory nerves. Oats provide mucopolysaccharides, which helps increase the lubricating fluids in bone joints, decreasing wear and tear.

~

*Makes about 1¼ cups
(10 fl oz/310 ml); serves 1*

~

*¼ cup rolled oats
¼ cup (2 fl oz/60 ml) water
1 large guava, peeled and chopped
1 apple, chopped
1 serrano chili, chopped
1-inch (2.5-cm) piece fresh turmeric*

Combine oats and water, soak 15 minutes. Strain and squeeze oats to extract all liquid, discard oats, reserving liquid. In a juice extractor, process remaining ingredients, then add to liquid. Mix well.

## Carrot and Parsley Juice
### (Bad-breath improver)
~

Bad breath can be the result of digestive problems, gum or tooth disease, or sinus/respiratory problems. This juice is a general tonic and cleanser due to the beta-carotene and chlorophyll it contains. It is especially helpful if the underlying cause of bad breath is the digestive system.

~

*Makes about 1 cup
(8 fl oz/250 ml); serves 1*

~

*2 oz (60 g) fresh parsley
1 oz (30 g) alfalfa sprouts
1 celery stalk with leaves, chopped
2 carrots, chopped*

In a juice extractor, process first the parsley, then the alfalfa, celery and carrots.

## Cranberry and Apple Juice
### (Bladder-infection fighter)
~

Cranberries have been found to help prevent the onset of bladder infection as well as to reduce its severity. As they are quite tart in flavor, the apple adds some sweetness.

~

*Makes about ¾ cup
(6 fl oz/180 ml); serves 1*

~

*2½ oz (75g) fresh or thawed frozen cranberries
⅔ cup (5 fl oz/160 ml) apple juice*

In a blender, combine cranberries and apple juice and blend until smooth. Strain into a serving glass.

*Carrot and Lime Juice*

## Salad in a Glass
### (Blood-pressure lifter)

~

This juice is like drinking a salad! It is full of potassium, which helps in the regulation of blood pressure and can improve excessively low blood pressure.

~

*Makes about 1¼ cups*
*(10 fl oz/310 ml); serves 1*

~

*1 small cucumber, chopped*
*1 apple, chopped*
*1½ celery stalks with leaves, chopped*
*1 ripe tomato*
*¼ bunch parsley*

Process ingredients in a juice extractor and mix well.

## Honey and Lemon Zinger
### (Bronchial elixir)

~

An excellent tonic to help reduce the congestion of bronchitis. The onion and honey liquid act as an expectorant, assisting in the breaking up and expelling of mucus. Honey soothes a sore throat, and lemon juice provides some vitamin C.

~

*Makes about ½ cup*
*(4 fl oz/125 ml); serves 1*

~

*½ large onion, finely chopped*
*3 tablespoons honey*
*½ cup (4 fl oz/125 ml) hot water*
*2 tablespoons fresh lemon juice*

Combine the onion and honey in a small bowl, cover and refrigerate overnight. (This mixture will keep up to 1 week and may be used as needed.) Combine 2 teaspoons of the onion liquid with the hot water and lemon juice.

## Orange and Blueberry Drink
### (Bruise reducer)

~

Blueberries and orange zest provide bioflavonoids, which help to strengthen blood vessel walls. The vitamin C in the orange works along with the bioflavonoids.

~

*Makes about 1¼ cups*
*(11 fl oz/340 ml); serves 1*

~

*Finely grated zest and juice of 1½ large oranges*
*7 oz (220 g) fresh or thawed frozen blueberries*

In a blender, combine all the ingredients and blend until smooth.

## Carrot, Cauliflower, Apple and Turmeric Juice
### (Cancer tonic)

~

This juice is not a cure, but it contains many nutrients that have been shown to help in the prevention of cancer. The beta-carotene in the carrot is an excellent antioxidant. Cauliflower is a member of the brassica family of vegetables, all of which have been shown to fight cancer. The apple contains ellagic acid, an anti-cancer compound, while turmeric contains curcumin, an antioxidant and anti-inflammatory compound.

~

*Makes about 1⅓ cups*
*(10 fl oz/310 ml); serves 1*

~

*2 medium carrots, chopped*
*½ apple, chopped*
*¼ small cauliflower, chopped*
*1¼-inch (3-cm) piece fresh turmeric*

Process all the ingredients in a juice extractor and mix well.

*Salad in a Glass*

## Super-antioxidant Juice
### (Cancer tonic)

~

This juice is not a cure, but the ingredients provide a hefty dose of antioxidants, which help rid the body of the free radicals that can increase the risk of cancer.

~

*Makes about 1¼ cups*
*(10 fl oz/310 ml); serves 1*

~

*2 medium carrots, chopped*
*½ medium beet (beetroot), chopped*
*1 celery stalk with leaves, chopped*
*1 oz (30 g) spinach*
*4 sprigs fresh parsley*

Process all the ingredients in a juice extractor and mix well.

## Pear and Alfalfa Heart Tonic
### (Cardiovascular tonic)

~

This drink provides soluble fiber to help reduce cholesterol levels; vitamin E, which is an antioxidant shown to reduce cardiovascular disease; and vitamin C. The chlorophyll in the alfalfa sprouts acts as a blood tonic and internal cleanser, and garlic assists in maintaining healthy blood pressure.

~

*Makes about 1 cup*
*(8 fl oz/250 ml); serves 1*

~

*1 clove garlic*
*¾ oz (20 g) alfalfa sprouts*
*1½ pears, chopped*
*½ teaspoon wheat germ oil*

In a juice extractor, process the garlic, alfalfa sprouts and pears. Whisk in the wheat germ oil.

## Apricot, Orange and Ginger Smoothie
### (Cholesterol reducer)

~

The fiber in apricots and oat bran helps reduce cholesterol levels by absorbing excess in the gastrointestinal tract. Ginger, onion and garlic also help, so use plenty of these in your cooking.

~

*Makes about 1¼ cups*
*(10 fl oz/310 ml); serves 1*

~

*5 dried apricots, chopped*
*¾ cup (6 fl oz/180 ml) water*
*juice of 1 large orange*
*2 teaspoons oat bran*
*1 teaspoon finely grated fresh ginger*

In a saucepan, combine apricots and water and boil. Reduce heat, cover and cook for 15 minutes. Cool, then combine liquid and remaining ingredients in a blender. Blend until very smooth.

## Spicy Green Corn Juice
### (Circulation stimulator)

~

This drink has a slight kick, due to the cayenne, which is a great tonic for sluggish circulation and a help with chilblains. Bok choy contains folate, which helps form all cells, including blood cells. Corn has some vitamin E, needed for the circulatory system.

~

*Makes about 1 cup*
*(8 fl oz/250 ml); serves 1*

~

*4 oz (125 g) fresh or thawed frozen corn kernels*
*6 medium bok choy (choy sum), chopped*
*1 medium apple, chopped*
*Pinch cayenne pepper*

In a juice extractor, process corn first, then bok choy and apple. Whisk in cayenne pepper.

*Super-antioxidant Juice*

## Prune and Apple Smoothie
### (Constipation preventer)

~

Prunes have long been used to promote elimination, and black pepper is a stimulant that helps to prevent constipation.

~

*Makes about ¾ cup*
*(6 fl oz/180 ml); serves 1*

~

*2 oz (60 g) pitted prunes*
*1 cup (8 fl oz/250 ml) water*
*good pinch black pepper*
*½ cup (4 fl oz/125 ml) apple juice*

In a blender, combine prunes and water, bring to a boil. Reduce heat, cover and cook 10 minutes. Let cool. In a blender, combine prunes and their liquid with remaining ingredients and blend.

## Papaya, Orange, Rose Hip and Cardamom Drink
### (Cough reducer)

~

Cardamom reduces coughs and bronchial problems, while rose hip contains vitamin C. Oregano also reduces coughs, and papaya contains beta-carotene and soothes a sore throat.

~

*Makes about ¾ cup*
*(6 fl oz/180 ml); serves 1*

~

*½ teaspoon cardamom seeds*
*1 rose hip tea bag*
*1 teaspoon chopped fresh oregano leaves*
*¼ cup (2 fl oz/60 ml) boiling water*
*12½ oz (385 g) papaya, peeled, seeded and chopped*
*1 orange, peeled and chopped*

Crush cardamom seeds and put in a cup with tea bag and oregano. Add boiling water and steep for 15 minutes. Strain and reserve liquid. In a juice extractor, process papaya first, then orange. Whisk in reserved liquid.

## Celery Root Juice
### (Cramp fixer)

~

Celery root and broccoli contain magnesium and calcium, nutrients that help to prevent leg cramps. The apple lightens the flavor, while the lemon juice provides vitamin C and prevents the celery root juice from discoloring.

~

*Makes about 1 cup*
*(8 fl oz/250 ml); serves 1*

~

*8 oz (250g) celery root (celeriac), peeled and chopped*
*or 8oz (250g) broccoli, chopped*
*1 medium apple, chopped*
*½ lemon, peeled and chopped*

Process the celery root, then the apple and then the lemon in a juice extractor.

## Pepper, Cucumber, Spinach and Apple Juice
### (Dandruff tonic)

~

This drink contains nutrients such as silicon, zinc, vitamin E and B vitamins, all of which help increase the health of skin and hair.

~

*Makes about 1 cup*
*(8 fl oz/250 ml); serves 1*

~

*2 oz (60 g) fresh spinach*
*1 small red bell pepper (capsicum), seeded and chopped*
*½ medium cucumber, chopped*
*½ apple*
*½ teaspoon wheat germ oil*

In a fruit extractor, process first the spinach, then the pepper, cucumber and apple. Whisk in the wheat germ oil.

*Prune and Apple Smoothie*

## Lemon Balm, Orange and Ginger Drink
### (Depression lifter)

~

For mild depression, lemon balm will help calm and lighten your mood. Orange juice has vitamin C and folate, a lack of which is thought to contribute to depression. Ginger and cinnamon are also mood lifters..

~

*Makes about ¾ cup*
*(6 fl oz/180 ml); serves 1*

~

*1 lemon balm tea bag*
*½ cup (4 fl oz/125 ml) boiling water*
*juice of 1 large orange*
*1 teaspoon finely grated fresh ginger*
*¼ teaspoon ground cinnamon*

Put tea bag in a cup and add boiling water. Cover and steep for 10 minutes. Remove tea bag and let cool. Add orange juice, ginger and cinnamon.

## Carrot and Green Bean Sugar Controller
### (Diabetes aid)

~

This is not a cure, but it may help with diabetes. Onions can help reduce blood sugar levels, while Jerusalem artichoke contains insulin, a type of carbohydrate that improves blood sugar control.

~

*Makes about 1¼ cups*
*(10 fl oz/310 ml); serves 1–2*

~

*2 medium carrots, chopped*
*3½ oz (105 g) green beans, chopped*
*¼ small onion, chopped*
*1 medium Jerusalem artichoke (sunchoke), chopped*
*½ apple, chopped*

Process ingredients in a juice extractor and mix well.

## Apple and Nutmeg Tummy Settler
### (Diarrhea easer)

~

Grated browned apple is an age-old remedy for diarrhea, and the slippery elm strengthens its effectiveness. Nutmeg helps to settle nausea and also diarrhea. Remember to drink plenty of water so you don't become dehydrated.

~

*Makes about ¾ cup*
*(6 fl oz/180 ml); serves 1*

~

*½ apple*
*½ cup (4 fl oz/125 ml) water*
*pinch ground nutmeg*
*2 teaspoons slippery elm*

Grate the apple, spread it on a plate and let sit for 30 minutes to brown. In a blender, combine apple and remaining ingredients and blend until smooth.

## Papaya and Mint Drink
### (Diarrhea recovery tonic)

~

A drink to help get you back on the road after a bout of diarrhea. Papaya is soothing and provides beta-carotene; yogurt and slippery elm help to restore bowel flora and normal function; and mint reduces spasms of the intestines.

~

*Makes about 1 cup*
*(8 fl oz/250 ml); serves 1*

~

*6½ oz (200g) papaya, peeled, seeded and chopped*
*2 tablespoons natural acidophilus yogurt*
*1 teaspoon chopped fresh mint*
*½ cup (4 fl oz/125 ml) water*
*2 teaspoons slippery elm*

In a blender, combine ingredients until smooth.

*Papaya and Mint Drink*

## Apple, Pear, Beet and Ginger Juice
### (Eczema aid)
~

Because the skin is an organ of elimination, rashes can indicate the need for improved toxin removal by the body. Beets help to promote liver function, which improves the elimination ability of the digestive system. The carotenes in beets also help to maintain good skin health. Ginger acts as an anti-inflammatory agent to help reduce the itchiness of eczema, while apple and pear are gentle on the system and provide soluble fiber.

~

*Makes about 1 cup*
*(8 fl oz/250 ml); serves 1*
~

*1 apple, chopped*
*1 pear, chopped*
*½ large beet (beetroot), chopped*
*½-inch (1.2-cm) piece fresh ginger*

In a juice extractor, process all the ingredients and mix well. Drink immediately.

## Blueberry, Orange and Cantaloupe Juice
### (Eye-health aid)
~

Some essential nutrients for eye health are bioflavonoids, which help strengthen and maintain blood capillaries, and beta-carotene for its antioxidant activity, which has been shown to help reduce the incidence of cataracts and other degenerative eye disorders. Vitamin C works with bioflavonoids and is also an antioxidant.

~

*Makes about 1¼ cups*
*(10 fl oz/310 ml); serves 1*
~

*¼ medium (12 oz/375 g) cantaloupe (rockmelon),*
*peeled, seeded and chopped*
*1 large orange, peeled and chopped*
*7 oz (250 g) fresh or thawed frozen blueberries*

Process ingredients in a juice extractor. Mix well.

## Orange, Lemon and Yarrow Drink
### (Fever reducer)
~

Yarrow is an herb that helps induce perspiration, which helps to break a fever. The orange and lemon juice provide vitamin C to boost the immune system. If you have a fever, drink plenty of fluids, including warm clear broths and diluted fruit juice.

~

*Makes about 1 cup*
*(8 fl oz/250 ml); serves 1*
~

*2 teaspoons dried yarrow*
*½ cup (4 fl oz/125 ml) boiling water*
*juice of 1 orange*
*2 tablespoons fresh lemon juice*

Put the yarrow in a cup and add the boiling water. Cover and let steep for 10 minutes. Strain and let cool. Combine the tea with the orange juice and lemon juice and mix well. Drink immediately.

## Pineapple and Ginger Juice
### (Flatulence reducer)
~

These combined juices are an excellent digestive aid. Bromelain, the enzyme in pineapple, assists in digestion, and ginger has long been used for its carminative, or wind-dispelling, quality.

~

*Makes about 1 cup*
*(8 fl oz/250 ml); serves 1*
~

*½ medium pineapple, peeled, cored and chopped*
*¾-inch (2-cm) piece fresh ginger*

Process the pineapple and ginger in a juice extractor and mix well.

*Blueberry, Orange and Cantaloupe Juice*

## Lemon, Dandelion and Artichoke Drink
### (Gallstone preventer)

~

These ingredients can stimulate the gallbladder and detoxify, which helps reduce gallstone formation. Artichoke and turmeric are choleretics; which means they increase bile flow, as does dandelion root. Lemon zest contains limonene, which helps dissolve gallstones, and psyllium helps absorb and remove wastes and excess cholesterol.

~

*Makes about 1 cup*
*(8 fl oz/250 ml); serves 1*

~

*2 teaspoons dried roasted dandelion root*
*¾ cup (6 fl oz/180 ml) boiling water*
*½ small artichoke*
*1 lemon, chopped*
*1¼-inch (3-cm) piece fresh turmeric*
*2 teaspoons honey*
*1 teaspoon psyllium husks*

Put dandelion in a cup with boiling water and steep 10 minutes. Strain and refrigerate until cold. Remove outer leaves from artichoke, trim ends of remaining leaves and cut into small pieces. In a juice extractor, process lemon, artichoke and turmeric. Combine with dandelion water and honey and whisk in psyllium.

## Cherry Juice
### (Gout tonic)

~

The flavonoids in cherries help lower uric acid levels in blood. It is uric acid that forms crystal deposits and creates gout inflammation.

~

*Makes about 1¼ cups*
*(10 fl oz/310 ml); serves 1*

~

*14 oz (440 g) pitted fresh or canned cherries, drained*
*½ cup (4 fl oz/125 ml) water*

In a blender, combine cherries and water and blend.

## Pineapple, Chili & Onion Drink
### (Hay fever fighter)

~

Chopped onion and honey is an age-old remedy to help break up and expel mucus. Onion contains bioflavonoid quercetin, which is a natural anti-inflammatory agent. Bromelain, the enzyme in pineapple, helps inhibit histamines, thereby reducing the allergy response. Chili helps desensitize airways to irritants.

~

*Makes about 1 cup*
*(8 fl oz/250 ml); serves 1*

~

*½ large onion, finely chopped*
*¼ cup (2 fl oz/60 ml) honey*
*¼ medium pineapple, cored, peeled and chopped*
*1 small serrano chili, chopped*
*⅓ cup (3 fl oz/80 ml) water*

Combine onion and honey in a small bowl. Cover and refrigerate overnight. (This mixture will keep in a refrigerator for up to 1 week.) In a juice extractor, process pineapple and chili. Add 2 teaspoons of onion liquid and water, mix well. Drink immediately.

## Blackberry Juice
### (Hemorrhoid treater)

~

Pears and oat bran contain soluble fiber, which provides bulk in the intestines and encourages elimination. Blackberries and cherries contain proanthocyanidins, which help strengthen the structure of veins. Both are important when treating hemorrhoids.

~

*Makes about 1 cup*
*(8 fl oz/250 ml); serves 1*

~

*4 oz (125 g) blackberries or pitted cherries*
*1 medium pear, chopped*
*3 teaspoons oat bran*

Process blackberries and pear in a juice extractor. Whisk in the oat bran.

*Blackberry Juice* (right)
*Ginger, Onion and Carrot Drink* (left; *see* page 104)

## Celery, Onion & Feverfew Juice
### (Headache reliever)
~

Onion is thought to decrease platelet aggregation, which in turn decreases headache pain. If you don't want to include the onion, try garlic capsules, which also play the same role. Ginger is an anti-inflammatory agent, and feverfew, taken daily, decreases the incidence of headache and migraine.

~

*Makes about 1 cup*
*(8 fl oz/250 ml); serves 1*
~

*2 celery stalks with leaves, chopped*
*¼ onion, chopped (optional)*
*½ apple, chopped*
*½-inch (1.2-cm) piece fresh ginger*
*4 fresh parsley sprigs with stems*
*1 tablespoon fresh feverfew leaves, finely chopped*

In a juice extractor, process celery, onion, apple, ginger and parsley. Mix well, then whisk in feverfew.

## Cantaloupe & Hawthorn Drink
### (High-blood-pressure tonic)
~

This drink combines an age-old remedy, hawthorn berries with cantaloupe and potato, which provide potassium. Potassium helps correct imbalances in the blood-regulating mechanism.

~

*Makes about 1¼ cups*
*(10 fl oz/310 ml); serves 1*
~

*1 tablespoon dried hawthorn berries, crushed*
*¼ cup (2 fl oz/60 ml) boiling water*
*½ medium cantaloupe (rockmelon), peeled, seeded and chopped*
*1 medium potato, chopped*

Put berries in a cup, add boiling water, cover and let steep 15 minutes. Strain, reserving liquid, cool. In a juice extractor, process cantaloupe and potato. Combine with hawthorn berry tea and mix well.

## Banana and Carob Shake
### (Hypoglycemia controller)
~

This drink has a low glycemic index factor, which makes it a slow-release energy drink. It helps to stabilize blood sugar levels and is beneficial for those who suffer with hypoglycemia.

~

*Makes about 1½ cups*
*(12 fl oz/375 ml); serves 1*
~

*1 cup (8 fl oz/250 ml) low-fat milk or fortified soy milk*
*1 ripe banana, peeled*
*3 teaspoons carob powder*
*2 teaspoons oat bran*
*2 teaspoons almond meal or ground almonds*

In a blender, process the ingredients until smooth.

## Red Papaya Soother
### (Indigestion preventer and reliever)
~

Both papaya's papain enzyme and pineapple's bromelain enzyme assist with digestion, and ginger is also an excellent digestive aid.

~

*Makes about 1 cup*
*(8 fl oz/250 ml); serves 1*
~

*½-inch (1.2-cm) piece fresh ginger*
*8 oz (250 g) red papaya, chopped*
*½ medium pineapple, peeled, cored and chopped*

In a juice extractor, process the ginger first, then the papaya and pineapple.

*Red Papaya Soother*

## Warm Peach and Honey Soother
### (Insomnia easer)
~

The tryptophan in milk stimulates the release of serotonin, a hormone that promotes relaxation. Chamomile is a calming herb that encourages restful sleep, and honey acts as a mild sedative. Peaches provide a touch of sweetness as well as beta-carotene.

~

*Makes about 1¼ cups*
*(10 fl oz/310 ml); serves 1–2*

~

1 chamomile tea bag
¼ cup (2 fl oz/60 ml) boiling water
4½ oz (140 g) canned peaches in natural juice, drained
½ cup (4 fl oz/125 ml) low-fat milk, warmed
1 teaspoon honey, or to taste

Put the tea bag in a cup and add the water. Let steep for 10 minutes. Remove the tea bag and pour the liquid into a blender. Add all the remaining ingredients and blend until smooth.

## Peppermint and Mango drink
### (Irritable-bowel-syndrome aid)
~

Peppermint tea is soothing to the digestive system, and mango provides soluble fiber, which helps to reduce the symptoms of irritable bowel syndrome. Acidophilus powder improves bowel flora by increasing the good bacteria present and reducing the disruptive unfriendly bacteria.

~

*Makes about 1¼ cups*
*(10 fl oz/310 ml); serves 1*

~

1 peppermint tea bag
¾ cup (6 fl oz/180 ml) boiling water
1 large fresh mango, peeled, cut from the pit and chopped, or 6 oz (185 g) frozen mango flesh
1 teaspoon acidophilus powder

Put the tea bag in a cup and add the boiling water. Cover and let steep for 10 minutes. Remove the tea bag and let the tea cool. In a blender, combine the tea, mango and acidophilus powder and blend until smooth.

## Pear, Fennel, Ginger and Mint Juice
### (Irritable-bowel-syndrome soother)
~

To soothe an irritable bowel, you need soluble fiber and calming foods and herbs. The pear in this drink supplies the fiber, while the fennel, ginger and mint all help to soothe and calm an unhappy digestive tract.

~

*Makes about 1 cup*
*(8 fl oz/250 ml); serves 1*

~

1 large pear, chopped
½ large fennel bulb, chopped
¾-inch (2-cm) piece fresh ginger
14 fresh mint leaves, finely chopped

Process the pear, fennel and ginger in a juice extractor. Whisk in the mint.

*Pear, Fennel, Ginger and Mint Juice*

## Cranberry, Carrot & Lemon Drink
### (Kidney stone preventer)
~

Cranberries are an excellent tonic for the urinary system. Dandelion is a natural diuretic, which helps flush the kidneys and relieves fluid retention. Carrot juice is also a good ingredient for internal cleansing.

~

*Makes about 1¼ cups*
*(10 fl oz/310 ml); serves 1*
~

*1 teaspoon dried roasted dandelion root*
*2 tablespoons boiling water*
*8 oz (250 g) fresh or thawed frozen cranberries*
*2 medium carrots, chopped*
*½ lemon, chopped*

Put dandelion root in a cup and add boiling water. Steep for 10 minutes. Strain and reserve liquid, cool to room temperature. In a juice extractor, process cranberries, carrots and lemon and combine with the dandelion liquid.

## Celery, Ginger & Feverfew Juice
### (Migraine tonic)
~

An unusual drink that helps prevent and relieve migraines. Feverfew is an excellent preventative; try to eat several leaves with bread daily. Ginger helps relieve nausea and cayenne pepper depletes substance P in sensory nerves, useful in pain control.

~

*Makes about 1 cup*
*(8 fl oz/250 ml); serves 1*
~

*½-inch (1.2-cm) piece fresh ginger*
*1½ medium apples, chopped*
*2 celery stalks with leaves, chopped*
*1 teaspoon finely chopped fresh feverfew*
*Sprinkle of cayenne pepper*

In a juice extractor, process ginger, then apples and celery. Whisk in feverfew and cayenne pepper.

## Minty Ginger Drink
### (Motion sickness reliever)
~

Ginger has long been used as an anti-nausea tonic and is invaluable for motion sickness. Fennel and mint are carminative herbs that soothe nausea and digestive upsets. Pack this drink in a thermos or airtight drink container and take it with you on journeys to sip along the way.

~

*Makes about 1 cup*
*(8 fl oz/250 ml); serves 1*
~

*1 fennel tea bag*
*1 cup (8 fl oz/250 ml) boiling water*
*¾-inch (2-cm) piece fresh ginger, grated*
*1 tablespoon finely chopped fresh mint*

Put tea bag in a large mug. Add the boiling water, ginger and mint. Let steep for at least 15 minutes or until cool. Strain and serve warm or cold.

## Fennel, Basil and Ginger Drink
### (Nausea reliever)
~

A drink that combines calming and anti-nausea herbs and spices to help reduce feelings of nausea and other stomach upsets.

~

*Makes about ¾ cup*
*(6 fl oz/180 ml); serves 1*
~

*5 large basil leaves, finely chopped*
*½ cup (4 fl oz/125 ml) boiling water*
*¼ medium fennel bulb, chopped*
*½-inch (1.2-cm) piece fresh ginger*
*Pinch ground nutmeg*

Put basil in a bowl, add boiling water. Cover and let steep for 10 minutes. Strain, reserving liquid, cool. In a juice extractor, process fennel and ginger. Add to basil tea and whisk in the nutmeg. Sip slowly.

*Minty Ginger Drink*

# Anti-inflammatory Orange Juice
## (Neuralgia reliever)

~

This drink has antioxidants that help reduce inflammation and pain of neuralgia, and B vitamins for a healthy nervous system.

~

*Makes about 1 cup*
*(8 fl oz/250 ml); serves 1*

~

*4 oz (125 g) chopped broccoli*
*2 oranges, peeled and chopped*
*1½ teaspoons grated orange zest*
*½ teaspoon wheat germ oil*
*½ teaspoon wheat germ*

In a juice extractor, process broccoli, then oranges. Whisk in zest, wheat germ oil and wheat germ.


# Apple, Apricot & Almond Shake
## (Osteoporosis reducer)

~

Dried fruit contains boron, needed for bone-building along with with calcium and magnesium. Milk and almonds are also excellent bone-strengtheners.

~

*Makes about 2½ cups*
*(20 fl oz/625 ml); serves 2*

~

*5 dried apples*
*7 dried apricots*
*1 cup (8 fl oz/250 ml) boiling water*
*1¼ cups (10 fl oz/310 ml) milk or fortified soy milk*
*¼ cup (2 fl oz/60 ml) ice-cold water*
*1 oz (30 g) unblanched almonds*
*½ teaspoon vanilla extract (essence)*

Put apples and apricots in a bowl and add boiling water. Let soak for 20 minutes. Drain fruit and cool. In a blender, combine drained fruit and remaining ingredients and blend until smooth.


# Carrot, Ginseng, Ginger and Parsley Tonic
## (Prostate-health drink)

~

This tonic has most of the nutrients needed for prostate health.

~

*Makes about ¾ cup*
*(7 fl oz/210 ml); serves 1*

~

*1 ginseng sachet or tea bag*
*¼ cup (2 fl oz/60 ml) boiling water*
*2 medium carrots, chopped*
*½-inch (1.2-cm) piece fresh ginger*
*2 sprigs fresh parsley with stems*
*1 teaspoon flaxseed oil (linseed oil)*

Empty contents of sachet or tea bag into a cup, add boiling water. Stir, cool to room temperature. In a juice extractor, process carrots, ginger and parsley. Combine with tea and whisk in flaxseed oil.


# Pineapple, Orange and Kiwi Fruit Juice
## (Psoriasis tonic)

~

Many people with psoriasis have a deficiency of digestive enzymes and folate. This drink supplies these in abundance, and psyllium helps absorb and eliminate any toxins. Drink this before meals.

~

*Makes about 1¼ cups*
*(10 fl oz/310 ml); serves 1*

~

*¼ small pineapple, peeled, cored and chopped*
*1 orange, peeled and chopped*
*1 kiwi fruit, peeled and chopped*
*2 teaspoons psyllium husks*

In a juice extractor, process pineapple, orange and kiwifruit. Whisk in psyllium.

*Pineapple, Orange and Kiwi Fruit Juice*

## Ginger, Onion and Carrot Drink
### (Sinus clearer)
~

This spicy mix achieves good results. Although strong in flavor, onion is an excellent decongestant and mucus expeller. Carrots provide beta-carotene, which helps in the repair and maintenance of mucous membranes. Ginger and wasabi both help to reduce inflammation and to clear the sinuses.

~

*Makes about 1 cup (8 fl oz/250 ml); serves 1*

~

½-inch (1.2-cm) piece fresh ginger
1 thin wedge onion, chopped
2 carrots, chopped
¼ teaspoon wasabi paste

In a juice extractor, process first the ginger, then the onion and carrots. Whisk in the wasabi.

## Lemon and Honey Drink
### (Sore throat soother no. 1)
~

This drink helps to reduce bacteria in the throat and to boost the immune system. Lemon juice contains lots of vitamin C, and garlic and honey are both antibacterial foods. Horseradish helps to reduce mucus congestion.

~

*Makes about ¾ cup (6 fl oz/180 ml); serves 1*

~

1 clove garlic
½ lemon, chopped
½ teaspoon prepared horseradish
1–2 teaspoons honey
½ cup (4 fl oz/125 ml) hot water

In a juice extractor, process first the garlic, then the lemon. Whisk in the horseradish, honey and hot water. Drink while hot.

## Orange and Sage Juice
### (Sore throat soother no. 2)
~

Sage is an anti-bacterial herb used to soothe a painful sore throat, and the vitamin C in oranges helps to prevent strep throat. Wheat germ oil contains vitamin E and essential fatty acids, while orange zest provides bioflavonoids.

~

*Makes about 1 cup (8 fl oz/250 ml); serves 1*

~

2 oranges, peeled and chopped
1 teaspoon finely chopped fresh sage
1 teaspoon grated orange zest
½ teaspoon wheat germ oil

Process the orange in a juice extractor. Whisk in the remaining ingredients.

*Orange and Sage Juice*

## Sage, Pineapple & Guava Drink
### (Tonsillitis soother)

~

Sage is an ancient remedy for sore throats, and pineapple is also known to relieve them. Guava supplies vitamin C, which boosts immune function, and carrot has beta-carotene, an antioxidant.

~

*Makes about 1¼ cups*
*(10 fl oz/310 ml); serves 1*

~

*10 fresh sage leaves, chopped, or 5 dried sage leaves, crumbled*
*¼ cup (2 fl oz/60 ml) boiling water*
*¼ small pineapple, peeled, cored and chopped*
*1 small carrot, chopped*
*1 small guava, peeled and chopped*

Put sage leaves in a cup and add the boiling water. Cover and let steep for 15 minutes. Strain and let cool. In a juice extractor, process the pineapple, carrot and guava. Combine with the sage tea.

## Cabbage and Carrot Juice
### (Ulcer soother)

~

This is not the best-tasting drink, but it really does help heal an ulcer as cabbage increases the production of protective substances in the digestive tract, carrot contains beta-carotene, which helps repair mucous membranes, and slippery elm provides a protective coating that lines the digestive tract and encourages repair. Add honey, if you like, and drink once or twice a day.

~

*Makes about 1¼ cups*
*(10 fl oz/310 ml); serves 1*

~

*14½ oz (450 g) cabbage, chopped*
*1 medium carrot, chopped*
*2 teaspoons slippery elm powder*

In a juice extractor, process cabbage and carrot. Whisk in slippery elm powder. Drink immediately.

## Berry Smoothie
### (Varicose vein preventer)

~

Berries contain flavonoids, which help to strengthen blood vessel walls. Ginger contains fibrin, which helps the body to resist varicose veins, while oat bran helps to prevent constipation, a contributing factor to varicosities.

~

*Makes about 1¼ cups*
*(10 fl oz/310 ml); serves 1*

~

*4 oz (125 g) fresh or thawed frozen blueberries*
*4 oz (125 g) fresh or thawed frozen raspberries*
*2 teaspoons oat bran*
*1 teaspoon finely grated fresh ginger*

In a blender, combine all the ingredients and blend until smooth. Stir in a little water or apple juice if needed to thin the consistency.

## Peppery Cucumber Juice
### (Wound healer)

~

Wheat germ oil provides vitamin E, needed for tissue repair. (You may prefer to take a vitamin E supplement instead of the oil if you don't like the taste.) The bell pepper provides vitamin C, needed for cell growth and tissue repair, and the chlorophyll in the parsley and cucumber skin also helps to heal wounds.

~

*Makes about 1 cup*
*(8 fl oz/250 ml); serves 1*

~

*½ oz (15 g) fresh parsley sprigs*
*½ medium red bell pepper (capsicum), chopped*
*1 small cucumber, chopped*
*½ teaspoon wheat-germ oil (optional)*

In a juice extractor, process parsley, then pepper and cucumber. Whisk in wheat germ oil.

*Sage, Pineapple, & Guava Drink* (left)
*Berry Smoothie* (right)

# General Index

# Ailment Index

# Guide to Weights
# & Measures

The conversions given in the recipes in this book are approximate.
The exact equivalents in the following tables have been rounded for convenience.

## Oven Temperatures

| Fahrenheit | Celsius |
|---|---|
| 125° | 52° |
| 150° | 65° |
| 175° | 80° |
| 200° | 95° |
| 225° | 110° |
| 250° | 120° |
| 275° | 135° |
| 300° | 150° |
| 325° | 165° |
| 350° | 180° |
| 375° | 190° |
| 400° | 200° |
| 425° | 220° |
| 450° | 230° |
| 475° | 245° |
| 500° | 260° |
| 525° | 275° |
| 550° | 290° |

## Weights

| Ounces (oz) | Grams (g) |
|---|---|
| 1 | 30 |
| 2 | 60 |
| 3 | 90 |
| 4 | 125 |
| 5 | 155 |
| 6 | 185 |
| 7 | 220 |
| 8 | 250 |
| 10 | 315 |
| 12 | 375 |
| 14 | 440 |
| 16 (1 lb) | 500 |
| 1½ lb | 750 |
| 2 lb | 1 kg |
| 3 lb | 1.5 kg |

## Liquids

| Cups/Tablespoons | Fluid Ounces | Milliliters |
|---|---|---|
| 2 tablespoons | 1 fl oz | 30 ml |
| ¼ cup (4 tablespoons) | 2 fl oz | 60 ml |
| ⅓ cup | 3 fl oz | 80 ml |
| ½ cup | 4 fl oz | 125 ml |
| ⅔ cup | 5 fl oz | 160 ml |
| ¾ cup | 6 fl oz | 180 ml |
| 1 cup | 8 fl oz | 250 ml |
| 1¼ cups | 10 fl oz | 310 ml |
| 1½ cups | 12 fl oz | 375 ml |
| 1¾ cups | 14 fl oz | 430 fl oz |
| 2 cups | 16 fl oz | 500 ml |
| 3 cups | 24 fl oz | 750 ml |
| 4 cups | 32 fl oz | 1 L |
| 6 cups | 48 fl oz | 1.5 L |
| 8 cups | 64 fl oz | 2 L |

First published by Lansdowne Publishing Pty Ltd
Sydney NSW 2000, Australia

This edition published by Simon & Schuster UK Ltd, 2011
A CBS COMPANY

SIMON AND SCHUSTER ILLUSTRATED BOOKS
Simon & Schuster UK
222 Gray's Inn Road
London WC1X 8HB

www.simonandschuster.co.uk

A CIP catalogue record for this book is available from the British Library

ISBN 978-0-85720-259-8

Text: Jan Castorina & Dimitra Stais
Publisher: Deborah Nixon
Production Manager: Sally Stokes
Project Coordinator: Joanne Holliman
Editor: Carolyn Miller
Photographer: Louise Lister
Stylist: Vicki Liley
Design: Deb Snibson, The Modern Art Production Group
Cover Design: David Eldridge, Two Associates

Set in Giovanni using QuarkXPress
Printed in Singapore by Tien Wah Press (Pte) Ltd